PRAISE FOR
BROKEN SEAS

"In **Broken Seas**, veteran journalist and seasoned sailor M̶a̶r̶l̶i̶
Bree has crafted a series of stories that prove t̶h̶e ̶ ̶ ̶ ̶ ̶s
stranger than fiction. A remarkable c̶ ̶"
— **Herb McCormick**, Editor of **Cru**
and Boating Editor of **The New **

"It is no accident that our history boc̶ ̶ ̶ ̶ ̶ ̶ ̶ ̶adventures of
the sea. Sailors and non-sailors are cap̶t̶ivated by nautical stories.
Marlin Bree's new book, **Broken Seas**, explains in gripping detail
tales from both the Great Lakes and the ocean. When reading this
book you will feel like you are on board during some of the harshest
calamities in recent history."
— **Gary Jobson**, World-class sailor and boating author

"Marlin Bree's new book **Broken Seas** will crank up your adrenaline and jump-start your pulse. Bree's prose puts you right in the
middle of these extraordinary true adventures. From crossing the
Pacific in a 10-footer to braving a November blow on Lake Superior,
this book will leave you with spray on your face, wind in your hair
and an insatiable itching to get out on the water. Don't miss it."
— **Yvonne Hill**, Editor of **The Ensign** magazine

"Marlin Bree's first-hand knowledge of monster waves and survival
has enabled him to vividly and accurately describe six true adventures in **Broken Seas**. This book details triumph and tragedy and is
a must-read for sailors, and even landlubbers will enjoy these amazing tales."
— **Chuck Luttrell**, Author of **Heavy Weather Boating Emergencies**

"**Broken Seas** is a pleasure to read. The seafaring adventures are
well researched, the characters and their struggles come to life, and
best of all...their roots are from the freshwater byways."
— **Capt. Thom Burns**, Editor of **Northern Breezes** sailing magazine

BROKEN SEAS

True tales of extraordinary seafaring adventures

MARLIN BREE

MARLOR PRESS

Saint Paul
Minnesota

BROKEN SEAS

ISBN-13: 978-1-892147-09-7
ISBN-10: 1-892147-09-2

*Printed in the United States of America
First Edition*

*Distributed to the book trade in the USA
by Independent Publishers Group, Chicago
Cover design by Mighty Media*

Library of Congress Cataloging-in-Publication Data

Bree, Marlin, 1933-
   Broken seas / Marlin Bree.--1st ed.
      p.cm
   Includes index.
   ISBN 1-892147-09-2
   1. Sailing. 2. Adventure and adventurers. I. Title

GV811.B67 2005
797.124--dc22   2004059712

MARLOR PRESS, INC.
4304 Brigadoon Drive
Saint Paul, MN 55126

*Dedicated
to*

**Loris
&
Will**

*My Own
Safe
Harbor*

BOOKS
BY
MARLIN BREE

WAKE
OF THE
GREEN STORM
A Survivor's Tale

IN THE TEETH
OF THE
NORTHEASTER
A Solo Voyage on Lake Superior

CALL
OF THE
NORTH WIND
Voyages and Adventures on Lake Superior

BOAT LOG
& RECORD
A Practical Record Keeper
for You and Your Boat

BROKEN
SEAS
True Tales of Extraordinary Seafaring Adventures

ALSO

BY GERRY SPIESS
WITH MARLIN BREE

ALONE
AGAINST
THE
ATLANTIC

CONTENTS

The lights begin to twinkle from the rocks:
The long day wanes:
the slow moon climbs;
The deep
Moans round with many voices.

Come, my
friends,
Tis not too late to seek a newer world.

– Ulysses

By Alfred,
Lord Tennyson

On Lake Superior's rocky north shore, broken seas crash and foam.

Photo / Clive Dudley

STORM HARBOR

WE'D SLICE DOWN THE BACKSIDE of one wave, and then another mound of water would playfully sizzle up and tap us to starboard. There'd be a whump-like noise, a little shove and a small explosion of white – and we'd bound up and down, and a little sideways.

Yes, the wind had definitely picked up. I braced myself in the cockpit of my home-built sailboat, *Persistence*. At the same time the breaker hit, my right hand on the tiller fed a little bow into the wave. We'd slide up and past the wave, down into the trough, and resume our ritual dance with the wind and water. *Persistence* was handling the building seas just fine.

I was enjoying myself on another solo sailing adventure on Lake Superior – I've been a boater on the Big Lake for many decades. This was where I wanted to be, on the northernmost arc of the world's largest freshwater lake, in a wilderness area as unchanged as when the ancient voyageurs paddled through on their way from New France. Around me was a panorama of sky, water and small islands.

I checked my GPS readout and saw we were

making 6.9 mph. crossing the Montreal Channel, a fine speed for a 20-foot centerboard sloop in Lake Superior's cross winds and waves. I'd have to be cautious: there are a lot of reefs out here and some of them are not all that well charted.

I was betting that with my Canadian nautical charts, my compasses (three) my depth sounders (one electronic, the other in the form of a swing keel that loudly let me know when it hit something), plus my Global Positioning System (GPS), that I'd find a refuge from the rising windstorm. A boater from Thunder Bay had advised me where to find a certain harbor inside a tiny island and showed me where it was on my nautical chart. Now I had to get off the lake.

My boat shouldered a blast of wind and gave a dip to leeward. Time to get the sail down. In my heavy nylon harness and lifeline, I lurched forward in the cockpit and dropped my reefed main and wound up my patch of jib on the roller furler. I fired up my 5 hp. Nissan outboard engine and, with an assist from the wind's fingers on my tall mast, we soared into a small channel. I was surprised that heavy winds had turned even the partly-sheltered channel smoky. Gray foam lay over its blue waters.

Carefully watching my GPS, I ran down the rocky edge of a lofty island, its flanks covered with dark-green fir trees and its base awash with waves and foam. Where was the entryway? A glistening patch of blue appeared between two cliffs: here was the cut I was looking for.

Suddenly, I was in another world – a quiet, peaceful harbor. Loon Harbor's hills and trees took the brunt of the blast.

I skimmed over the harbor's waters. When I figured I had a good anchorage, I threw out my two Danforths and watched them sink through the clear water to the bottom. I gunned the engine in reverse, firmly setting the hooks.

Home for the night, I unclipped my safety harness for the first time today and ducked below into my tiny cabin. My senses were welcomed by the smell of coffee, wood, and var-

In an island harbor, Persistence bobs gently in gin-clear waters.

nish. I slammed the heavy wood hatch shut above me and wearily sank down into the starboard quarterberth. I'd be safe enough through the night, unless the wind switched.

Outside my boat, shadows lengthened; the sun turned red and was setting. I watched its orb rush across the water and disappear.

Odd. I sat up straight.

It took a moment to understand what was happening: my boat and I were gliding back and forth in the wind. The sun was a constant beacon, but my moving boat was a world of constant motion. It was a matter of perspective. I reached out my forefinger to trace the sun's movement on the port light.

Time passed, the lowering sun set and the far shore grew dark. There was no moon. I was in the midst of elemental forces, alone in this unquiet darkness.

Things come out in the dark.

I struck a match and the flame from my candle lantern flickered softly yellow, illuminating my tiny world. Memories grew large.

For many years, I've been a boater. I've had the privilege of voyaging over the big waters of the world and I've had adventures and met wonderful people.

The sun was gone, but now I had my own internal beacon.

Here in my solitary harbor, I was surrounded by friends and memories.

Slowly, I picked up my pen and began to write.

— Marlin Bree
Onboard *Persistence*
On Lake Superior

ONE

TEN FEET
ACROSS
THE
PACIFIC

INTRODUCTION

MISTS SHROUDED THE GRAY SEAS OFF THE LIZARD as *Yankee Girl* searched for land. Aboard his 10-foot sloop, Gerry Spiess had been working his way toward Falmouth, England, encountering not only a thick fog but strong tidal currents that could sweep his little plywood boat into the treacherous reefs of Cornwall's coastline. He'd listen for the Lizard's fog horn, a long blast followed by a short one, then start up his outboard engine and head directly toward the sound. After 10 minutes, he'd turn off the engine, listen and take a new bearing.

Suddenly, the fog lifted. Rising above the cliffs was the sparkling Lizard point and beyond, green fields.

The ex-schoolteacher breathed a sigh of relief. He had ended one of the most remarkable voyages in history by piloting his home-built boat 3,800 miles across the stormy North Atlantic Ocean to England to set a new world's record for the smallest boat to cross from West to East.

Left, Yankee Girl with skipper Gerry Spiess arriving in England after a record-breaking crossing of the North Atlantic. Top, the skipper sails triumphantly in Falmouth harbor.

Two years after his 1979 North Atlantic voyage, he wanted to sail the same little boat again. This time the challenge he picked was to cross the world's largest ocean.

It would be a monumental voyage of 7,800 miles to Sydney, Australia, across the Pacific Ocean.

He shoved off from Long Beach, California, hoping to quickly pick up the South Pacific's steady and balmy trade winds. His first port of call, Honolulu, Hawaii, beckoned to the west.

But the Pacific had turned cold and treacherous.

17

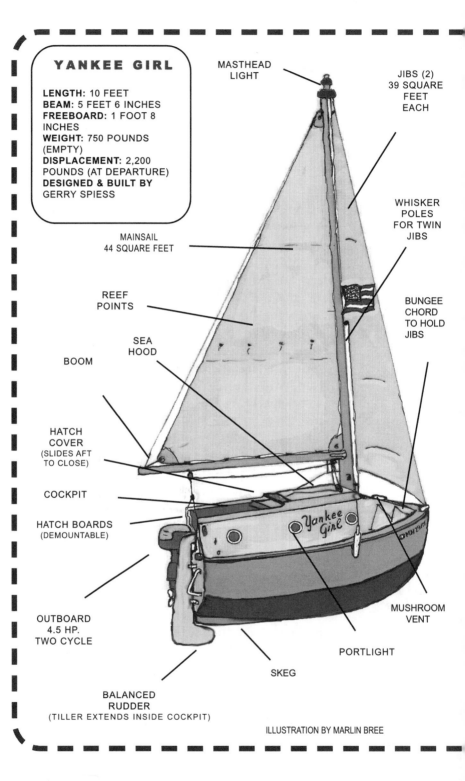

YANKEE GIRL

LENGTH: 10 FEET
BEAM: 5 FEET 6 INCHES
FREEBOARD: 1 FOOT 8 INCHES
WEIGHT: 750 POUNDS (EMPTY)
DISPLACEMENT: 2,200 POUNDS (AT DEPARTURE)
DESIGNED & BUILT BY GERRY SPIESS

MASTHEAD LIGHT

JIBS (2) 39 SQUARE FEET EACH

WHISKER POLES FOR TWIN JIBS

MAINSAIL 44 SQUARE FEET

REEF POINTS

BUNGEE CHORD TO HOLD JIBS

BOOM

SEA HOOD

HATCH COVER (SLIDES AFT TO CLOSE)

COCKPIT

HATCH BOARDS (DEMOUNTABLE)

OUTBOARD 4.5 H.P. TWO CYCLE

MUSHROOM VENT

PORTLIGHT

SKEG

BALANCED RUDDER (TILLER EXTENDS INSIDE COCKPIT)

ILLUSTRATION BY MARLIN BREE

TEN FEET
ACROSS THE
PACIFIC

The remarkable voyage
of Gerry Spiess
and *Yankee Girl*

A FULL MOON HAD ARISEN over the South Pacific Ocean and in its silvery light, ominous big rollers were forming and breaking. Long waves with white breakers were beginning to overhang the small sailboat and slam hard into *Yankee Girl's* transom, giving her nasty shoves.

As Gerry Spiess threw open the hatch, a chill wind brushed his face and he saw that the waves were starting to run confused and were piling up.

A splash of spray hit him – the water was remarkably cold.

It wasn't supposed to be like this.

Voyaging in the South Pacific was supposed to have sunshiny days in warm trade winds, with tropical nights ablaze with stars. But this trip was turning nasty.

It was the evening of the ninth day, and, the waves were rearing up to overshadow the 10-foot sloop. He had entered the convergence zone, where a cold current runs down from Alaska and meets the warm central current. Big rollers were starting to form and break.

When the wind changed direction, it had created two sets of waves. One set of waves was running 8 to 12 feet; the other waves ran at more than 8 feet.

Worse yet, the wave trains were starting to collide as the wind came around.

Slamming his hatch shut, Gerry slumped back into his cabin and the warmth of a sleeping bag. He was thankful that he had decided earlier to take down all sails and run under bare poles – a standard procedure for rough weather. But he knew he was in for a rough night.

There was a heavy thump. Suddenly, sheets of water poured through the closed hatch. Startled, Gerry looked up to see a small Niagara flooding inside the cabin. The water felt surprisingly cold.

Hawaii lay more than 1,800 miles away – and was looking increasingly distant.

A FOLLOWING WAVE had overrun *Yankee Girl,* buried her in water, and turned her into a submarine with only her mast sticking out. The water pressure had blasted through the sliding hatch closure.

Moments later, she fought her way free of the wave, but Gerry knew his boat was in danger. *Yankee Girl* was heavy laden.

The steep seas, closely bunched, were so bad that even running under bare poles wasn't working. She couldn't take many more waves over her transom.

Timing the waves, Gerry threw back the hatch and crouched on the wet deck as *Yankee Girl* pitched below him.

In the moonlight, he could see a big wave roaring toward him. He managed to close the hatch below him., but there was not a lot to hang onto. He lunged forward on the cabin top to the mast, in the peculiar scuttling motion he had to use on a tippy boat with a five-and-a-half foot beam

With one hand on the mast, he inserted a foot on the starboard shroud and chain plate and crouched down. The wave roared over the transom and overran the boat, splashing him.

Gerry felt the boat careen momentarily to one side. *Yankee Girl* hesitated, then righted herself.

From his position, he could reach forward with one hand to pull out the jib, which was lashed under shock chord along the bow's starboard side.

Coolly, he leaned forward with one hand to pull out the sail and hank it onto the forestay. He tied the jib halyard to the sail and crossed the jib sheet to the opposite side. Minutes later, he had the mainsail unlashed along the boom.

Wet and chilled, he tumbled back into the cockpit and hoisted the deeply reefed main and the jib. After throwing the tiller to the opposite side, *Yankee Girl* obediently turned, pointed her bow into the wind and heaved to.

He had done it. The effect was astonishing and immediate.

It seemed as if the ocean suddenly had gone calm; *Yankee Girl* slowly would move forward, then fall off, stall out, move a little backward, then resume her motion forward. Instead of being bashed in her broad, flat transom by the heavy waves, her pointed bow speared into the breakers and shoved them to one side. With her sails up, she had balance and direction.

Gerry sighed with satisfaction. Heaving to was one of the heavy weather maneuvers *Yankee Girl* excelled at. She did not do well lying to a sea anchor, for she would sail forward and overreach, making the anchor useless in waves. But with her v-shaped hull, and long keel, she could heave-to steadily, even in broken seas, and work easily with the waves, like a little fishing bobber.

A last look around and Gerry slammed the hatch shut, dogging it down.

He had done all he could for his little boat. Now she'd have to look after him.

AT DAWN, he sensed something was different. *Yankee Girl's* motion had changed.

His muscles aching from the long night and his skin itching from his damp bunk, Gerry threw open the hatch and blinked in the early morning light.

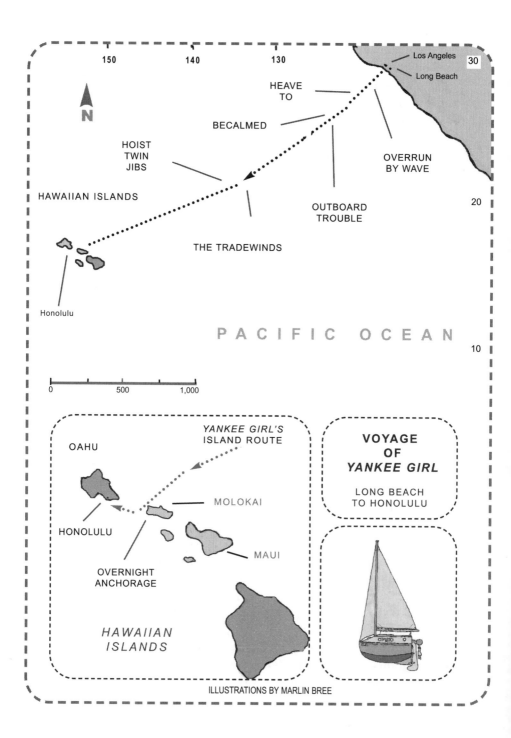

150　　　　140　　　　130

N

HEAVE
TO

BECALMED

HOIST
TWIN
JIBS

HAWAIIAN ISLANDS

Los Angeles

Long Beach

30

OVERRUN
BY WAVE

20

OUTBOARD
TROUBLE

THE TRADEWINDS

Honolulu

PACIFIC OCEAN

10

0　　　　500　　　　1,000

YANKEE GIRL'S
ISLAND ROUTE

OAHU

MOLOKAI

HONOLULU

MAUI

OVERNIGHT
ANCHORAGE

HAWAIIAN
ISLANDS

VOYAGE
OF
YANKEE GIRL

LONG BEACH
TO HONOLULU

ILLUSTRATIONS BY MARLIN BREE

The sun was high in the sky, but the Pacific spread lumpy seas to every horizon. Gone were the breaking seas of last night, but *Yankee Girl's* sails were beginning to slat and flutter.

They had gone from too much wind to not enough.

Becalmed.

Gerry scratched his salt-soaked beard and peered over the transom – his engine was still on its motor mount. It had been repeatedly doused as waves had overrun the boat. It must have been battered by thousands of breakers; he'd heard it shudder and bang under the wave's battering. More than once during the night, he wondered if it'd been torn off.

But it was a tough two-cycle outboard, and, he'd always had great luck with the two-cycles, even on his stormy North Atlantic crossing, where his elderly 4-hp. Evinrude had been beaten by cross waves and repeatedly doused. Behind him was a brand new 4.5-hp. engine.

These engines always fire up, Gerry thought, as he pulled the starting cord through to get the gas up.

Then he yanked another time – *hard.*

Nothing happened.

HE TRIED AGAIN AND AGAIN, but the outboard would not start. It would spin through, but not catch and fire up. He began to perspire and not just from the exertion.

Had something broken in the storm? Without an engine, he would be in deep trouble. He needed the small outboard to get back on schedule in the calms and to get into harbors. It was a critical part of his strategy.

More tries at starting the engine would not help – it was time for a new tactic. He took his hand from the starting chord, his arm already starting to ache.

What was the problem? The first guess came quickly. Electrical, probably. That was always a good guess on boats. Out of curiosity, he raised the throttle arm and peered beneath. The engine had a shut-off, or kill, button at the end of the throttle arm. If you pushed the button, the engine stopped.

He saw what was causing the problem. Somehow, the waves had shorted out the kill switch.

With a needle nose pliers from his repair kit, he snipped its wires – hopefully bypassing the problem.

He crossed his fingers and hauled hard on the starter cord. With a whuff of smoke, the little two-stroke started up and soon settled into a raspy idle.

H E SET HIS COURSE TOWARD HAWAII, running his engine just barely turning over at a fast idle – at a stately cruising speed of around 2.2 knots (2.53 mph.) – which he maintained almost nonstop day and night for the next 6 days.

To refuel, he'd unscrew the filler top of his six-gallon main gas tank, pour in gas from one of the gas cans from the bilge, screw back the top, and continue cruising – without stopping his engine. He did shut his engine off several times to change the engine's single spark plug – cheap insurance, he figured.

The slow, but consistent running was part of his crossing strategy. It took patience, but gave him great gas mileage. At the speed he ran the engine, the two-cycle single cylinder engine only used a fraction of a gallon per hour. That meant one gallon of pre-mixed gas and oil would last more than seven hours. A 24-hour day's run would consume only 3.5 gallons. He carried 54 gallons of pre-mixed gas on board, most of it in the bilges, down low for ballast.

At low speeds, *Yankee Girl's* power cruising was effortless, but noisy. When he was piloting the boat, he sat in the aft bunk, with his head near the transom and the outboard, or when he slept in short periods, he had his head just a few feet from the engine. He found he couldn't get away from the outboard's noise – particularly annoying for a wind sailor.

He became aware of another problem. Inside the cabin, Gerry sniffed the air to discover the faint, but unmistakable smell of two-cycle smoke.

He sat up straighter. If that were coming back into the open hatchway, there might be something else: the deadly invisible, odorless killer – carbon monoxide gas.

With a light following breeze, but not enough wind to power up the sails, there was no escaping the problem that heavier-than-air carbon monoxide was finding its way into his tiny cabin and down into the bilges.

He tried keeping the hatch open only one or two inches, which was only a partial solution, he realized. He also found he couldn't sleep well or for very long. The engine droned on.

He began to yearn for the trade winds.

H E DID NOT FEEL the first, gentle gust, but noticed that his engine speeded up from its usual fast idle. Odd, Gerry thought and he looked up to see his sails starting to draw.

His boat was a wind ship again.

It was the beginning of the third stage of his trip to Hawaii and the one he looked forward to the most. He shut down the little outboard by choking it off and let the trade winds fill his sails and carry him to the islands.

Soaring along in the trades was a wonderful feeling. *Yankee Girl* was clearly enjoying herself, bowling along majestically on a peaceful, rolling sea. The Pacific was starting to live up to its legends.

In crossing the North Atlantic, he came to rely on his twin jibs to pull him along, but now he could try out his 180-square-foot spinnaker, set on two poles. The big red chute ballooned up in front of him and *Yankee Girl* picked up speed.

But it was not a comfortable ride with all that canvas up. *Yankee Girl* seemed not to handle or steer well: she would yaw a bit and need course correction. Frankly, she worried him.

After several hours, Gerry hauled the spinnaker down and again hoisted his twin jibs. In this arrangement, his two 39-square foot jibs were both poled out from the bow to resemble two odd-shaped triangles. By sheeting each jib separately, he could control the sails perfectly from the safety of his cockpit.

Now *Yankee Girl* steered herself in the trade winds, without his hand on the helm and with perfect control.

He noted with satisfaction that his speed was only a two-tenths of a knot slower than with the spinnaker.

Now in her stride, the little boat began to eat up the miles. With the twin jibs pulling her along like small ponies, her daily run increased. Some days, she'd do 85 nautical miles – some days, 95.

Gerry relaxed in the open cockpit, enjoying his fine pocket cruiser in the trade winds and bright sunshine – the South Pacific he had hoped for. As he peered into the water, he saw that its color had changed to a deep indigo blue. He reached over and cupped a handful just to admire its beauty.

For his navigation, he had two Davis plastic sextants. This included a sextant he bought for $20 and had used to cross the Atlantic. He mostly used the $20 one because he liked it so much.

From his navigational calculations, he knew he was nearing the Hawaiian Islands, so he turned on his transistor radio and listened to a broadcast from a Hawaiian station. He had an air-craft radio on board and he could hear pilots somewhere in the skies checking with air controllers in preparation for landing.

As one flight high in the sky came nearly overhead, Gerry called to it via his aircraft radio. He told them where he was and gave them his GPS coordinates, but after several tries, the pilots could not make the tiny boat out in the waves below. Gerry watched their contrails etch white against the blue sky.

The jet would land in Honolulu in 40 minutes.

He'd be there in about five days.

OFF IN THE DISTANCE, the islands of Hawaii rose to greet him, first the Big Island, then, Maui, and finally Molokai. Blue peaks emerged out of a light hazing of mist. He could see their green tips from a long way off.

It was his first sighted landfall in nearly 2,500 miles and the islands were right where his plastic sextant told him they'd be.

Gratefully, Gerry steered around the northern edge of Molokai to a small beach with a sand bottom and good protection from the trade winds.

It was late afternoon when he dropped his small anchor and

began to make preparations for his landing at Honolulu. He did not want to come through the Kaiwi Channel at night on his way to Oahu and he needed to make preparations after many days at sea.

With *Yankee Girl* bobbing in the blue waters, and, Molokai's green hills nearby, Gerry enjoyed the Hawaiian breezes with the hatch open.

The land smelled wonderful, but there was much to do.

From the bow area, he brought up some empty gas cans, which he filled with seawater, so that his boat would have the right trim. Since *Yankee Girl* did not have any permanent ballast, but relied upon stores for weight below, he needed to maintain the right load in the bilges.

He checked his main gas tank and figured he'd have enough gas left to make it in to Honolulu. No need to top it up: he'd sail in the beautiful trade winds and he'd only need to run his engine for maneuvering.

He shook his head: there was a lot of housekeeping to do, but that'd have to wait. Down below in the bilges, salt water had begun to rust some of his cans of food and supplies. The inside of his boat was damp because of the water he had taken inside through the hatch closures.

He had already lost his flannel-lined sleeping bag, which had gotten soaked. He had tried to dry it out, but on a small boat, there was no room and after three days it began to smell badly – like old tennis shoes. His only recourse was to toss it overboard. For warmth, he had huddled under several blankets because the early part of the voyage had temperatures lower than expected in the cold California current, which swept a third of the way to Hawaii

But now tropical breezes wafted over him. He had a supper out of a can – his favorite at sea, Dinty Moore stew – and fell asleep, exhausted.

It was a good night's sleep, in the shadow of the great island, his boat bobbing gently in protected blue waters.

Tomorrow would be his homecoming.

THE VHF RADIO inside the grass-thatched bar in Honolulu had been squawking transmissions as I listened intently for Gerry's messages. Gerry's destination was the Waikiki Yacht Club. I had flown over with my wife, Loris, and my son, Will, to greet him.

Some members of the media had been out in the channel in chartered boats to film *Yankee Girl's* triumphant arrival and were back, looking somewhat green. "God that was rough," one of them said. "What must it have been like in that little boat?" It had been a wild ride, no question of it. The Kaiwi Channel lies between the islands of Molokai and Oahu and funnels both trade winds and currents into fast-moving, high waves. At times, even some local sailors don't venture out into the rough Kaiwi Channel.

But it was a sleigh ride for Gerry heading past Diamond Head. Speeding along on only one jib, he sat on the starboard side of the cockpit, bracing himself in the rollers, and waving to members of the press.

He was jubilant.

He and his boat were headed home.

IN THE WAIKIKI YACHT CLUB BAR, I kept hearing Gerry's voice on the VHF radio. *Yankee Girl* had arrived outside the breakwaters and he seemed impatient to come in.

I knew why. He was waiting for someone to guide him into the harbor and that someone was sitting at a table in front of me.

"I need to finish this hand," my skipper told me. He was playing cards. As I was to learn, these were the islands, and, some things were done on island time.

Minutes later, the card game ended and our skipper swallowed the last of his gin and tonic. "Let's go," he said with a friendly wave and we walked along the Ali Wai small boat harbor quay to his trawler.

The diesel fired up and the trawler headed out majestically. It was not hard to figure out where *Yankee Girl* was — a small squadron of boats circled and surrounded her.

In Honolulu's harbor: A triumphant arrival

Gerry was standing in the cockpit, rolling back and forth in their wake.

From the trawler's bridge, I called down to Gerry and then waved. Gerry seemed to squint, but did not recognize me. I tried the radio, but got no response.

I shouted, "Follow us."

Yankee Girl snicked into gear. Gerry began following the trawler into the harbor, escorted by some of the inquisitive boats in a sort of informal parade.

Gerry was allocated the guest-of-honor berth at the club – right in front of the open-air restaurant. The word had spread around the island and people had gathered to see the remarkable little boat and its builder-skipper.

After his long sea voyage, Gerry had to be helped from the boat. As he walked, I saw that he was supported on one side by his wife, Sally, and on the other by his dad, Lou.

"Marlin," Gerry said, after staring at me. "You made it."

He looked around: "Where's Will?" He had always been fond of my young son.

"He's here," I said, pointing. Walking in Gerry's footsteps was our 11-year-old son, ever-so-carefully staying out of his friend's way, but never far, either.

"Hey!" Gerry said, delighted.

In the hours ahead, Gerry began to get his land legs back and I marveled at how well he looked – sun tanned and healthy, with a dark beard.

Despite being in his boat all this time, he had seemed to achieve a small sartorial miracle: he appeared nattily dressed in clean, pressed clothing, just as if he had just stepped from one of the beautiful Honolulu hotels.

Once again, it was Gerry's incredible knack for detail that was paying off: he had packed a plastic canister with clean, fresh clothes just for this occasion. He had put them on this morning.

I was impressed. It was a small, but significant detail, and, only one in a chain of events and details he had carefully thought through.

All of his preparations had paid off on this voyage. He had crossed the biggest single leg of his journey across the world's biggest ocean and he had set a record for doing so in the smallest boat ever.

Moreover, his little boat had handled beautifully, both in storms and in the trade winds. He had averaged 65 nautical miles per day (74.75 statute miles), an outstanding run for any boat much less one only 10 feet long. He had reached 95 nautical miles (109.25) in his best day's run.

He had estimated that it would take him 36 days to make his crossing. He did it in 34.

Nothing had broken on the "little girl," as he came to refer to her and she had done everything he had asked of her.

Yankee Girl had once again proven herself.

There was no question in Gerry's mind that she easily could carry him the rest of the way across the wide Pacific.

EPILOGUE

Fully rigged with her hatch open, Yankee Girl is on display in a Minnesota Historical Society exhibit. For exhibit purposes, the rudder, tiller and engine have been removed and the hatch boards are also out.

Photo/ Marlin Bree

YANKEE GIRL seems to float on a calm blue sea under brightening skies, with her mainsail set. Her hatch is open, invitingly, and from somewhere, there is the suggestion of a trade wind coming up. She looks wonderful.

The little boat is no longer on the South Pacific, but in a diorama created for her by the Minnesota Historical Society. For a number of years, this remarkable little boat has been on display at the Minnesota Historical Society, in the *Minnesota A to Z* exhibit (*Yankee Girl* was under Y.) Millions of visitors have admired her and marveled at her design and construction.

She tilts just a bit to one side, as if heading off invitingly. As a visitor now, I stand behind the exhibit's barrier and peer over *Yankee Girl's* open transom to look inside the little boat once more.

I see some familiar sights. There is Gerry's gear – his plastic water bottle, his navigation equipment, his electronic equipment and some of his clothing. To my nostalgic eye, she looks like her skipper has just stepped off and she is just waiting for him to come back and take the helm.

Clearly, she is ready and able to head off on another voyage.

What an adventure the two of them had.

After Honolulu, she and Gerry headed southwest to Fanning Island, a tiny atoll, and from there to American Samoa and Fiji.

They ended up with a hero's welcome in Sydney, Australia, after making a record crossing. It was a feat for the record books – *Yankee Girl* was the smallest vessel ever to cross the South Pacific.

I talked to Gerry several times about why he made the Pacific voyage, especially after all the hardships of the North Atlantic crossing. He told me that he really liked his little boat and that *Yankee*

Girl "sailed like a dream." She was, he said, "so good he just wanted to sail her some more."

Not only could she pick up her skirts and move well downwind with her twin jibs, but with her sloop rig, she could point high into the wind and tack where her skipper wanted her to go. She was a real boat, despite her tiny size, and a real sailor.

He had enormous pride in her. She was his creation. He had designed and built her, as well as sailed her, to many world records and maritime acclaim.

The Minnesota Historical Society exhibit of *Yankee Girl* is no more, but *Yankee Girl* herself lies somewhere in its vaults as a protected treasure. She will not sail again, for Gerry donated her to the Society and to the people of Minnesota. She is resting now, off the terrible oceans of the world and residing not many miles from the little Minnesota lake where she was born and tested.

Though she's gone from sight and will never put her bow into another wave, her adventures still fire the imagination of sailors everywhere.

What she and her sailor accomplished rank among the immortals of seafaring tales.

(For further details on Gerry Spiess, Yankee Girl, and the trans-Pacific voyage, see Author's Notes)

Photo: Painted photo by M.J. Humprey, owned by the Cook County Historical Society

THE
OLD MAN
AND THE
INLAND
SEA

Photo / Clive Dudley

PROLOGUE

ALONG THE NORTHWESTERN EDGE of Lake Superior, the North Shore of Minnesota grows scenic and bold. Dark ridges of the Sawtooth Mountains soar like turrets amid green pine and spruce while at the water's edge, Lake Superior rages against a dark, reef-strewn shore.

A chill wind was up and rustling the pine branches as I turned my 4 x 4 off Hwy. 61 onto a steep road to stop in Hovland, a tiny village located 20 miles south of the Canadian border. Beyond the bluffs, I could see whitecaps. Superior's waves were crashing onto the shore, lofting layers of spume that wet my glasses and chilled my face.

I stared out into that menacing world of broken sea and sky. It was hard to imagine a man in a small, open boat setting out from here during an oncoming November ice storm, trying to find a missing friend.

The rescuer was an old man, an immigrant from Norway who had fished these waters for many years, and he knew what to expect.

He went anyway.

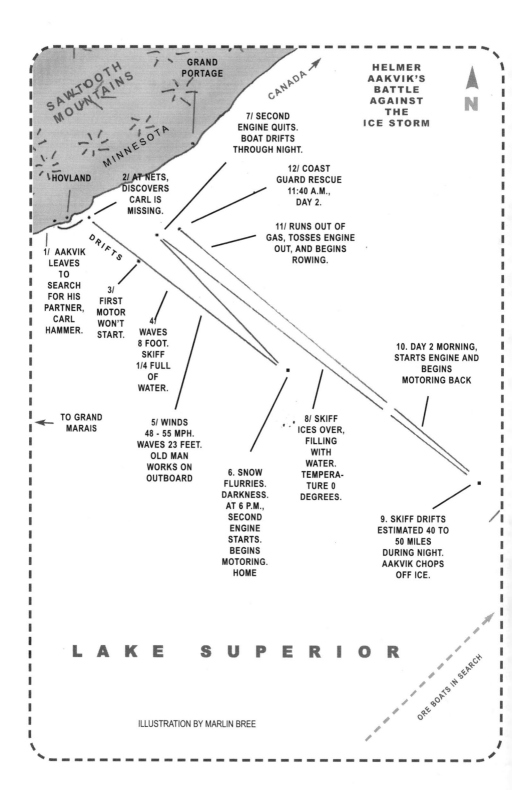

Photo/ Irene Malner

*Bow detail of North Shore skiff similar
to that used by Aakvik and Hammer*

OLD MAN

AND THE

INLAND
SEA

Helmer Aakvik's daring
rescue attempt
during an ice storm

L AKE SUPERIOR'S CHILL NOVEMBER WATERS were an ominous
slate gray and the lake was steaming with fog banks 40-
feet high. The wind was building out of the north-northwest as
Carl Hammer slipped his 17-foot wooden skiff into the water.
With the ease of a practiced boatman, he started his outboard
engine, and donned his canvas gloves. He was wearing a heavy
twill jacket with a quilted lining, and quilted twill trousers. It
was old gear, but well tested from the days when he worked on
the big ore boats. It'd keep the chill out of his 26-year-old's
bones.

He squinted at the wind, making his eyes tear up. The lake
didn't look like the weather would hold and waves were building in the offshore wind, but he wouldn't be long.

Photos above and left / Irene Malner

The boat house "boat slide" once ran down from the top of this bluff (above) to a rock-strewn waterfront. The slide allowed Aakvik and Hammer to launch their skiffs in the water's edge. Left, a smiling Carl Hammer, when he worked on the ore boats. Below, Helmer Aakvik in ice-covered oilskins with his open, wooden skiff.

Photo of Aakvik at right:
Painted photo by M.J.
Humprey, owned by the Cook
County Historical Society

He had his nets set only a mile-and-a-half offshore. He'd be out there before any storm came up, pick his nets, and get back quickly – just as he'd done thousands of times before.

There was no need for special precautions. It was 7 a.m., November 26, 1958, the day before Thanksgiving.

A T 8:30 A.M., Helmer Aakvik peered out the window of his three-room frame house not far from the bluffs overlooking Superior. The lake was steaming hard, a bad sign, and though he could not see them, he knew waves were kicking up further out.

He had already made his decision: he would not go out today.

The 62-year-old Aakvik settled down at his kitchen table to enjoy a second cup of strong coffee when a neighbor, Elmer Jackson, came trudging over. The back door opened with a blast of wind.

Jackson was blunt: "The young fellow is still out on his boat."

Aakvik looked up, troubled. The storm that was coming on was one of the worst kinds with an offshore wind from the north-northwest. He abruptly put down his coffee cup. "Call the Coast Guard," he said.

As he turned to leave, Jackson looked at Aakvik carefully and shook his head. "Just don't you go out."

G RABBING A JACKET and a cap, the Old Man walked down the winding path to the bluff's edge. There was a steady wind knifing of the northwest and, even in the protection of the rocky ridge behind him, the temperature was dropping. This was late November in the North Country; soon there'd be ice and snow.

On a near-vertical rock ledge jutting above the lake, he came to the ramshackle wooden fish house that he and Hammer shared. In the open end of the shed, he could see that Hammer's boat was gone. Spruce trees swayed ominously below in the onshore breeze.

He ducked back inside the wood shack and checked around. Sure enough, the young fisherman had helped himself to Aakvik's gas supply. The borrowing was OK – they shared supplies all the time in this close-knit Norwegian community.

The problem was that Hammer had a new outboard engine that used a different ratio of oil to gas in the fuel than Aakvik's.

The Old Man had an old Lockport and an elderly Johnson, but Hammer used a newer Johnson, which needed about a half a quart of oil mixed in five gallons of gas. Aakvik's old two-cycles required *twice* that amount of oil, and a too-heavy oil-gas ratio would gum up the young fisherman's carburetor and foul his spark plugs, stalling his engine.

He peered into the can, then swirled it around. He could see the drops of water on the surface. His gas was old and had accumulated water condensation. The old man's normal routine was to filter the water out of the gas so that it didn't freeze in the lines and kill the engine.

Hammer hadn't filtered his gas.

THE OLD MAN HURRIED BACK into his house and carefully dressed himself in layers of wool: socks, underwear, pants and shirt. Wool was the key to survival on Superior because it could keep him warm even when it was wet.

Over his wool, he put on his heavy rubber fisherman's suit, adding rubber boots, wool mitts and a sheepskin helmet. Aakvik never went out on that lake, winter or summer, without a good set of oilskins. Oilies were part of the equipment you needed for survival on Superior, especially late in the season when the famed "Witches of November" came calling.

He told everyone in his broken English, "they saved your life."

A LITTLE PAST 9 A.M., THE Old Man stood atop the rock outcropping over the slide. His 17-foot-long boat was tied to a wooden slide about 30 feet above the water, located high above the shoreline rocks.

Mercifully, the wind was blowing from the northwest, off the land and not from the water. Today there would be no problem launching the skiff.

The slide consisted of three trimmed tree trunks, each about 8- to 10-inches in diameter, and more than 40 feet long. As he attached a wire cable to his skiff's bow, the Old Man paused for a moment to throw a hatchet into his boat. Then he added two more pieces of equipment: an old wooden fish box that weighed almost 50 pounds and 50 fathoms of rope.

Ready to launch, the Old Man used a winch to lower his skiff down the boat slide into the dark waters. As he hefted himself aboard, the little skiff bobbed up and down a little to welcome his familiar weight. The Old Man felt at home.

His wooden boat was built along the lines of a North Atlantic dory, with a raked bow, slab sides and a flat transom. But his North Shore skiff was more heavily constructed. It had a heavy wooden v-shaped chine bottom, strong sawn ribs, a beam of 5 feet, with freeboard of a little less than 2 feet.

A really good skiff reminded the Hovland fishermen of boats from "the old country" – a high compliment. Like the Norwegian small boats operating in icy fjords, a Superior boat had to deal with big water. Its sharp bow was designed to split oncoming waves rather than trying to plow through them and have enough flare to lift the boat up so it didn't founder when running downwind.

At more than 20 years old, the Old Man's skiff was beyond a North Shore fishing boat's normal working years. It was tired: it had punched through countless waves, survived many storms, and had been dragged countless times up the boat slide with a full hold of fish. Moreover, it had rot in some of the bottom planks and the screws holding some of the planks to the frames felt a little loose.

But the Old Man had faith. His skiff had taken him out and brought him back every time.

THE FIRST BLASTS of the offshore wind sliced into him once he left the protection of the shore. Even dressed in his oilskins, the Old Man felt its bite. Out here, the wind was coming up sharply and the seas had started to build.

He'd have to hurry. The temperature was about 6 degrees above zero, and, it was dropping.

Atop a wave, he saw the first marker buoy flag and moments later, he could make out a string of bobbing buoys strung out in a row, their line bending in the wind and the waves.

But Carl Hammer was not there.

In the mounting waves, Aakvik made a run alongside the line, being careful not to foul his propeller on the nets.

One thing was certain: Hammer had not tied his boat to one of the marker buoys. These buoys were held securely by heavy rock anchors and if a fishing boat had engine trouble, the fisherman could hang on to a buoy to await rescue.

At the end marker buoy, Aakvik scanned the horizon. Out here, the big lake was alive. Away from shore, the waves continued to build and his small boat bobbed up and down.

He held his cupped hands to his eyes to give him better vision. Still no sign of Hammer or his skiff.

The Old Man pulled his boat alongside the final buoy, grabbed it for a moment, and turned off his engine.

And waited.

A LONG THE BLUFFS ON SHORE, the watchers with binoculars scanned the broken seas. The heavy rollers of Superior were high and mean now, with waves rearing into the lake's notorious "square rollers."

Visibility was poor, but the wind was coming up and blowing the fog around in patches. Someone shouted that he had seen someone moving alongside the nets.

Word had spread. The village knew that the Old Man had gone out to bring in The Kid.

Someone recognized Aakvik, his old boat bounding up and down in the waves, and hanging with his hands onto a buoy.

Minutes passed and they saw his boat move away from the nets. From the way his boat was handling, they could tell he was drifting, without power.

A AKVIK DELIBERATELY was moving with the waves and the wind. He figured that The Kid must have had a problem with his motor and that by drifting without power, the Old Man would be carried by the wind and waves in the same direction.

He prayed he'd be in time.

The wind speed was about 38 mph. He went down into the trough of one wave, then upward. His boat perched high atop a big breaker.

He did not know how high the waves were, but moving walls of water surrounded him and they were growing.

He tried to figure the speed and direction his partner was drifting. He had to hurry, so he started his engine and began running downwind, steering clear of the crests

When he was about seven or eight miles out, he let his engine idle atop a wave for one last look around for his missing partner. At this height, he could see for miles atop the tumbling seas, but there was no sign of Hammer.

The waves whistled loudly as they roared past his skiff. He realized he'd never heard them that noisy before.

There was little more for him to accomplish. For his own safety, it was time to head back toward shore.

He looked around to get his bearings, but in the fog, he could not see the tall headlands of home. That was all right, for he knew an old fisherman's trick: Since he had been going downwind, now he'd simply reverse himself and go upwind.

But that would mean that he'd have to turn his boat around and plunge directly back into the face of the mounting wind and waves.

Suddenly, the roaring outboard started to splutter, then die.

In the eerie silence, the Old Man turned to his engine.

It was white with ice.

I T WAS THE LOCKPORT. He had been using the elderly outboard without its cover, as he usually did. The entire engine had been splashed with spray and the water had frozen.

He wound the starting chord, pulled out the choke and turned up the throttle to start. He gave the chord a hard pull . The old engine wheezed several times.

Again and again, he ran through the starting drill. But the ice-encrusted engine would not start.

He sat back for a moment, weary, but thankful he had the foresight to bring his spare engine onboard. The newer 14-horsepower, two cylinder Johnson two-cycle lay in the floor-boards.

It would not be easy changing engines. In the storm-wracked seas in a pitching boat, he'd have to start by wrestling the heavy Lockport off the transom.Timing his movements between the waves, he unscrewed the clamps that held the Lockport to the transom and grunted: the outboard was frozen to the boat.

He partly stood up, hefted his weight against the hundred-pound engine, felt the ice break, and, leaned over to grasp the power head. He slammed and twisted, finally pulling hard and the old outboard came up, dripping water. He wrestled the slippery engine to one side and slid it into the bottom of the boat. In the bilge, the partly frozen water sloshed ominously. He picked up the newer Johnson, carefully lifting the dripping outboard in his arms, cradling it like a baby. Slowly, he slid the Johnson prop-first over the stern. There could be no mistakes now. One slip and the engine could fall to the bottom of the cold lake. Without power, there'd be no way back.

He braced himself to lower the power head onto its clamps. With a final slide through his partly frozen mitts, the outboard was on the transom and the small boat reacted to the extra weight and drag by cocking broadside to the wind. He tightened the clamps.

He wiped his face and discovered that perspiration had turned to ice. His hat had a rime of white around it.

He snicked the outboard's gear into neutral, pulled the choke button, twisted the throttle to the starting position, and yanked hard on the starter chord. There was not even an encouraging whuff, or, slight backfire.

Despite his efforts, his most dependable, newest engine wouldn't start. It had lain in the icy bilge water too long.

I N HIS T-35 JET TRAINER, Major Leo Tighe anxiously scanned the surface of stormy, wind-churned Superior. It would be almost impossible to pick out a small boat in the white caps, but still he had to try.

A slower flying plane, such as a C-47, would have been better on this mission, but the Duluth airport was already too iced up for it to take off.

A hit-and-run snowstorm had come up from nowhere, racing with unusual speed out of the west, and had dumped 13 inches of snow on the ground. Cold rain and sleet turning to ice had blanked the airport and the rest of the Midwest.

He had been lucky to get in the air.

Riding with him in the back seat was Lt. Gerald Buster. Flying in a north-south search pattern, they were buffeted with strong winds. More than once they came closer to Superior's outstretched fingers than they cared to.

"There!"

Major Tighe had spotted something in the waves below. He circled.

At 2 p.m., about 20 miles from shore, they saw a tiny, white-colored boat.

On their first pass, it looked like it was under power. The man in the boat's rear seat was paying no attention to their low-flying jet.

They circled again, this time lower yet, and saw that the man's engine wasn't putting out any wake, nor was the boat making any progress in the waves.

The boat was rolling broadside to the wave trains – a dangerous position. It looked like the man was in trouble, but he wouldn't look up or signal to them. The boat and the man were white.

Suddenly it dawned on Major Tighe that they were both ice-covered.

He circled the small craft again and again until a radar station on shore could get a fix on the position and relay the information to the Coast Guard.

Low on fuel, he returned to the Duluth air base. There wasn't anything else he could do from the air.

Silently, he said a small prayer.

ALL THAT LONG AFTERNOON, the skiff drifted with the wind and the waves while the old man labored over his balky engine. The waves were increasing in size, the wind was gusting louder than before, and he was moving further from shore.

A rogue wave reared over the boat, swamping it. His small boat was a quarter full of water.

Desperately, he bailed – but his boat was not buoyant enough and was riding too low in the water.

He moved forward to the bow and laid his hand on his old Lockport. He felt twinges of regret wash over him: it had been his fishing partner for many years. He'd taken it to the Hovland blacksmith shop many times to have it welded up. There was a bond between the old outboard and the Old Man. Like the old boat, it had soul.

With reluctance, he threw it overboard.

The motor hit the water and sank instantly. In the waves, there was not even a ripple where it once had been.

His skiff was lighter now by more than a hundred pounds. The Old Man saw the freeboard lift an inch or two in the bow. He began bailing again, trying to keep pace with the spray and spume that came aboard. His strategy was working.

When the water level was down to the floorboards, he turned his attention again to his one remaining engine.

He had to concentrate, for his life depended on that old outboard. Even when a jet fighter flew close overhead, he could only glance upward a moment. There was nothing they could do beyond reporting his position.

Somehow, he had to fix his engine. He did not have any tools with him – just an ax. He took off his gloves, baring his skin to the frozen metal, and twisted the gas line off by hand.

No gas was coming out – his line had frozen. There had been too much water in his gas as well.

The old fisherman thought a moment and stuck the gas line in his mouth. The raw rubber, soaked in gasoline, made him gag.

He kept it in his mouth, checking from time to time. After about a half an hour, he blew hard on one end. The ice block had melted in his mouth and popped out.

The line was free.

He tried to move in his boat, but his heavy boots were stiff with the cold and ice and one of them had split at the knee. Water began to trickle in.

Grimly, the Old Man remembered his fishing days in Alaska, where he had a neighbor who had to chop off his frozen toes with an ax. He wondered if it would come to that.

He had been at work on the boat and the outboard all afternoon. As he looked around him, he saw the short November day was growing dark.

He reattached the gas line to the engine and hauled hard on the starter chord.

With a roar, the old two-cylinder Johnson came to life.

HE HEADED FOR A SHORE HE COULD NOT SEE. He knew if he steered into the waves and wind, he'd end up somewhere along the coast.

But to get back, he had to steer into oncoming waves that were running hard. The 20-foot-high seas at times seemed to dwarf his boat.

The old skiff was taking a terrible pounding. Powering into the onrushing breakers, it would spear an oncoming wave, lift its bow partly, then stop nearly dead, shivering with the effort, again and again. The planks were flexing and they looked like they were separating. The screws holding them to the frames were pulling out. Water was coming in at an alarming rate, faster than he could bail it out.

There was nothing left to do but turn off the engine. When the engine quit running, the boat stopped pounding itself apart.

but the wind howled across his open boat and the white-crested growlers reared toward him.

Without power, his boat was cocked sideways to the waves. Breakers slopped in over the gunwales.

Reaching forward, he picked the rope out of the half-frozen slurry in the skiff's bilge and tied it to the sturdy wooden fishing crate. He grunted as he hefted the 50-pound crate over the side. With a splash, it sank part way into the waves, receding from his drifting boat.

When he felt a tug on the rope, he tied the line off the bow. The old skiff's bow swung around and began riding to the waves with her bow cocked at a slight angle to them. It was her best sea-keeping position.

His improvised sea anchor was working.

Night was coming on. The temperature dropped further and ice continued to grow on the skiff and the Old Man.

He had done all he could. Now he could only bow his head at the growing fury of the storm.

B ACK IN HOVLAND, the families were growing desperate. They could look out at the broken seas and imagine the ordeal of their men in the open boats.

They shared a sense of helplessness. "What could you do on shore?" Helmer Aakvik's wife, Christine, wondered aloud.

The sheriff had been called, but snow and high winds kept his floatplane from searching the storm-filled lake.

From Grand Marais, the Coast Guard's small boat ventured out to search, but it had to turn back when its engine lost power. Its gas line had begun to freeze up.

About 20 miles away, the big steel Coast Guard cutter, *Woodrush,* which was finishing its season at Isle Royale, got an emergency call. It responded by steaming into the teeth of the storm toward Hovland .

In the meantime, the Coast Guard sent out another, more seaworthy lifeboat. When the 36-foot lifeboat fought its way into Hovland, it was riding 6- to 8-inches lower in the water because of the ice that had covered the boat. The Coast Guard sailors reported that they had been fighting a Number 6 Sea, whose waves averaged 15 feet in height.

Chopping off ice, the lifeboat started a search up and down the shoreline, trying to estimate where the lost fishermen might have drifted. The lifeboat had no radar and the men had to search for the missing fishermen visually – an almost impossible job in the spray, ice and high waves. By evening, when they called off their search, the wind howled at nearly 50 mph..

The *Woodrush* kept on station, but temperatures fell to near the zero mark. The winds were increasing and so were the seas. Ice was building on its topsides, making even the big steel cutter dangerously topheavy and in danger of capsizing. Several times, the *Woodrush* had to return to harbor for its crew to chop off the ice.

Darkness came early. Along the shore in the little fishing community, people prayed that the Old Man and the Kid, each huddled alone in their open boats, would survive the long night.

H E HAD BEEN OUT MORE THAN SIXTEEN HOURS and he had nothing to eat or drink. His eyebrows were laced with ice and his eyes were burning orbs from the spray. His unprotected face was painfully cold. His foot where the boot had cracked and water had entered was growing numb. Worse, his mind was growing slack with fatigue.

In his wooden seat, he could only watch helplessly as waves came like dark walls out of the night. They rose high and crashed into the old boat and he could feel its agony as it wracked forward and sideways in the waves. Spray continuously slopped over its bow and froze. His boat was icing up.

If ice built up too much, he knew a small boat would get top heavy and roll over in the waves. Thankful he had taken his hatchet along, the Old Man reached forward and began chopping ice off his boat.

His mind drifted during the long night. He wondered what had happened to Carl. In his rush to check the nets that morning, The Kid probably just wore his usual work clothes, so he didn't have oilskins to protect him from the spray. He probably figured he was just going out for a quick dash to the nets and then back again, as he had done so many other times. He didn't carry a hatchet.

The Old Man thought of Carl with nothing to chop away the ice as his boat began lying lower and lower in the water and getting top heavy as spray came aboard and froze.

The Old Man bent his head into the wind.

His partner's end was probably quick, or he prayed it was. Carl probably just slumped down and went to sleep, worn out with cold and fatigue.

In these seas, his boat probably turned sideways into the waves, and top heavy with ice, it rolled over. That would have been the end.

The Old Man came alert. It would be so easy to slump in his little boat, bend his head down to his chest, as if in prayer, and let the motion of the skiff rock him into slumber.

But to sleep was to die.

Off in the distance, he could make out flashes of light bouncing off the tall headlands of Hovland and Chicago Bay. That would be his rescuers, but there was no way to tell them that he was further out from shore. A lot further.

He discovered he was no longer cold. The chill that he felt earlier was gone and he was suffused with warmth. His foot no longer ached and that was because it was numb. He probably had frozen it.

His skiff was covered with ice. When he looked down, he saw his oilskins also were coated in ice. His feet were encased in ice also; even his fingertips had icicles hanging from their tips.

The ice encapsulation was what was keeping him warm. It sealed up his oilskins with an extra layer to keep out the surf spray and the wind.

At some time during the night, the moon came out. The Old Man paused to admire the beauty of the spray by moonlight. It glistened white, surreal and ethereal around him.

He also saw something else gleaming white in the water.
Ice surrounded his boat.

THE LIGHT AROUND HIM BRIGHTENED, slowly, almost imperceptibly. The Old Man knew at last his long night was ended. It was the dawn.

The lake was covered with heavy steam – a light gray haze that hid what was below. But the wind had calmed somewhat. So had the seas.

He scanned the horizon to get a bearing on which way to head home, but he couldn't catch a glimpse of the high, dark hills above Hovland.

The Old Man had nothing to eat. He was tired, stiff, and he hurt. One foot was numb, possibly frozen.

Still he waited patiently. When the weak sun began to rise out of the water in the east, he'd have his bearing. He'd swing to the northwest and head home.

His boots were frozen to the bottom of the boat and he couldn't move forward to chop the ice in the front of the skiff. The ice cover had grown: the bow glistened white with ice a foot thick.

Somehow, he had to move.Cracking ice chunks off his oilies, he painfully managed to turn around to partly face his transom. His outboard was sheeted with ice he saw that ice had coated the flywheel.

The rope wouldn't fit in the starting pulley on the motor. The starter rope was frozen hard.

His hands were thick with ice, so he knocked his hands together, and then took off his mitts. Cautiously, he hammered the ice off the outboard and with his uncovered hands, he painfully worked a starter rope strand into flexibility.

Carefully, he wound two strands around the metal starting pulley. He kept his fingers moving so they would not freeze to the metal. The strands just fit, and, hopefully he put his mitts back on his numb hands. He waited a moment, said a silent prayer, and yanked. The engine chuffed into life with a puff of blue smoke.

The Old Man turned his boat toward home.

The skiff plowed slowly into the oncoming waves. He found that the bow was so heavy with ice that it lifted slowly, and at times, the boat barely maintained its buoyancy. The skiff rode eight inches lower in the water because of the ice's weight.

One tall wave could come aboard and sink them.

Carefully steering, he nursed his engine along for about six hours. When he was within sight of land, and only six or seven miles from shore, his outboard stalled and quit.

He checked his fuel supply. Out of gas.

FOR A MOMENT, he thought he was out of luck, too. His feet were frozen to the floorboards, so he could not stand or even reach forward with his ax to chop ice. Coated with ice, his boat rode too low in the water to stay afloat much longer.

The Old Man hated what he was about to do, but he had no choice. Loosening the setscrews that held it to the transom, he hefted the Johnson and watched dismally as the outboard slipped beneath the waves.

It was lost forever, but his boat was lighter.

He still had his oars, but he could not use them. His mitts had stiffened into icy claws.

The water was amazingly close to where he sat. It wasn't gray in color anymore, just a bluish white. Waves moved past, indicating that it wasn't totally frozen, though chunks of ice surrounded him and bumped into the boat.

He thought about his problem. He could drag his mitts in the water until they thawed, put them on and carefully fold them around his oars until they froze in place.

Then he could row.

The shoreline, he thought, was tantalizingly close. He could not give up.

IT WAS THANKSGIVING DAY. The *Woodrush* widened its search to criss-cross the area, but as the Coast Guard cutter plowed through one bank of fog and into another, its weary crew grew increasingly worried. The temperature hovered around zero degrees and there was ice in the water. Even if the two men had survived the cold and the ice, the rough lake easily could have taken down their small boats.

The cutter's motor grumbled on, its bow parting the waves and banging into the ice chunks while the shivering watch crew scanned the hungry seas.

"There!" someone yelled.

Off in the distance, something white and ice-covered bobbed up above the layer of lake steam.

As they steered nearer, they could make out a what looked like a person's head. His face and beard glistened with frost and his hat was coated with white. His clothing was encased in ice.

He rode low in a nearly swamped boat that was a itself block of ice.

It was the Old Man.

H E HAD NOT HEARD THEM APPROACH. Suddenly, he saw the looming bow of the Coast Guard's cutter headed directly toward him. He blinked, halfway thinking it was a delusion, until the steel bow nudged his boat with a bump.

He tried to get up, but he was covered with ice from head to toe and frozen to his wooden seat. His feet remained frozen to the floorboards.

The Coast Guard crew members came alongside the Old Man. With care, they managed to chop him free and lift him out of his skiff. When he was aboard, they fed him hot coffee – his first drink in 29 hours.

They tied a rope around the skiff's eyebolt and tried to tow it home. But the old boat was so heavy with ice and so weak after its battle that it only lifted its bow a little and then went under. They had to cut the rope as it sank quickly down into the dark waters.

As they came into Hovland's harbor, cheering rolled across the waves.

The Old Man looked around, amazed. "There must

have been a hundred people there," he recalled.

Though he was having trouble moving, he still shrugged off offers of help. "I can still walk," he said. "I'm no cripple."

He protested when he was placed on a stretcher and given a preliminary examination by a doctor. He did gulp down an egg sandwich and drink a pint of hot coffee. The doctor wanted to rush him to the hospital in Two Harbors. "As if I needed a hospital," the Old Man snorted. "I only froze two toes."

He declined a helicopter ride, insisting on riding sitting up in the ambulance. At the hospital, he was treated for frozen toes and frostbite. His hands were swollen from being exposed. A doctor pronounced him as being in excellent shape, with normal blood pressure.

From his hospital bed, he said there was no question in his mind if he'd make it to shore. He'd get home "even if I had to paddle to Grand Portage."

One news reporter asked him if he prayed to his God for help during the long night. "No," he allowed, "there's some things a man has to do for himself."

But few words were as sweet to the Old Man as those of his neighbor, Elmer Jackson, when he came to visit. Before the Old Man went out on his long search, Jackson had worried about him and the oncoming ice storm.

The Old Man had promised his neighbor: "Don't you worry, the Old Man will be back."

In the hospital, Elmer Jackson came to the his bedside and said, respectfully:

"You are a man of your word."

AAKVIK

HELMER MEIR   MARIE CHRESTINE
8 — 18 — 1896   4 — 17 — 1905
1 — 11 — 1987   12 — 19 — 1989
HOME FROM THE CRUEL SEA AND
NOW IN A PEACEFUL HARBOR.

EPILOGUE

I HEADED OFF HWY. 61 going north and climbed in third gear into the hills overlooking Lake Superior until I reached a small cemetery. It was located in the midst of a high, grassy meadow, surrounded by stately pine trees. The sun was down at a slant in the late afternoon, casting long shadows into the grass – and onto the small granite tombstones.

It was not difficult to find the final resting place of the Old Man, near the forest's edge. Today, a light wind swept through the boreal forest, gently rustling the pine needles and sweeping onto the clearing with a north woods' scent.

His headstone was simple carved granite, recording that he had been born 18 August 1896 and had died 11 January 1987. In the upper left was a ship's steering wheel and a small saying had been carved at the bottom of the stone:

Home from the cruel sea and
in a peaceful harbor

I bowed my head in respect to the Old Man and looked at the earth below my feet.

I knew what was down there: Helmer was resting in a plain wooden coffin, fitted with rope handles. His name had been carved on the coffin lid, along with a compass rose.

The Old Man had requested a small addition to his handbuilt coffin. He wanted it fitted with a keel, like a proper boat.

That was so he could, as he put it, "steer a straight course to the stars."

For further information on this story and North Shore fishermen and their boats, please refer to Author's Notes.

THE

LOST

SCHOONER

Afloat after being underwater for more than a century: the Alvin Clark

PROLOGUE

NEARING DUSK, the setting sun painted the weathered wooden stockade a golden color. Jutting out in startling black against the sun's red orb were two sharply raked masts that soared nearly 100 feet into the sky. It was the old schooner I was searching for: the *Alvin Clark* – the so-called Mystery Ship from 19 Fathoms.

She had a remarkable history. Built in 1846, the *Alvin Clark* had sunk in a squall with the loss of her captain and two crewmen. More than a 100 years later, she had been found remarkably intact and well preserved, brought to the surface with heroic effort by amateur sports divers, and triumphantly exhibited as a private museum ship.

The next morning, I was first in line to view this vessel that had been built before the Civil War. In awe, I walked her decks, admired her lines, marveled at her spars and rigging, and clambered down in her hold. I was in frank admiration of this historic ship and the men who sailed her.

Over the years, the memory of the Mystery Ship remained with me. She was a ship with an incredible story of death, courage and heartbreak – and she was the most exciting, oldest, and most significant recovered shipwreck in North America.

One day at a diving conference in Minneapolis, I was reminiscing with a friend about the *Clark*.

"They plowed her under," he said.

"I can't believe it!"

I was astounded. A beautiful and historic vessel couldn't end like this.

"She's broken up and underneath a land fill," he emphasized sadly. *"They built a shopping center over her."*

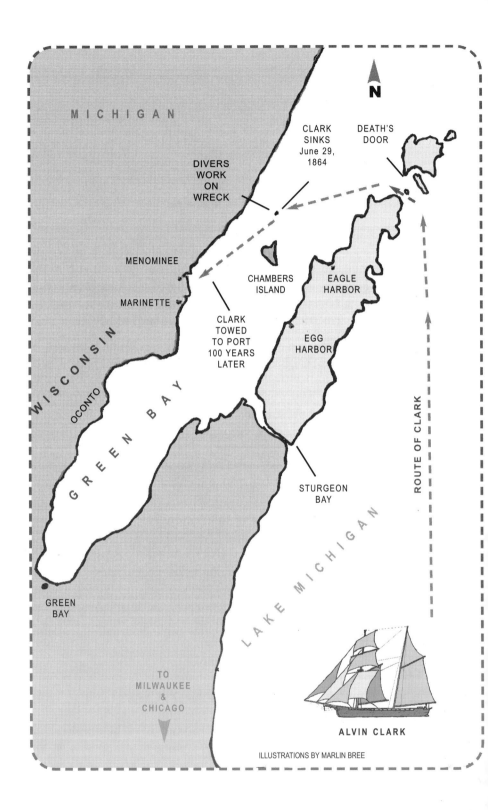

MICHIGAN

N

CLARK
SINKS
June 29,
1864

DEATH'S
DOOR

DIVERS
WORK
ON
WRECK

MENOMINEE

CHAMBERS
ISLAND

EAGLE
HARBOR

MARINETTE

WISCONSIN

CLARK
TOWED
TO PORT
100 YEARS
LATER

EGG
HARBOR

OCONTO

G R E E N   B A Y

STURGEON
BAY

ROUTE OF CLARK

GREEN
BAY

L A K E   M I C H I G A N

TO
MILWAUKEE
&
CHICAGO

ALVIN CLARK

ILLUSTRATIONS BY MARLIN BREE

THE
LOST
SCHOONER

The triumph and tragedy
of the 1846 *Alvin Clark*

I T HAD BEEN A WARM DAY IN LATE JUNE, 1864, when the *Alvin Clark* coasted past the eerily named Death's Door Passage to the north of Wisconsin's Door Peninsula, and entered the wide sweep of Green Bay. The topsail schooner had been reaching easily behind a southwesterly wind and heading under full sail for Oconto, WI.

She was a centerboard vessel, whose swing keel could be raised or lowered to make it possible for her to wiggle into undeveloped ports and shallow harbors to pick up and deliver cargoes. With her sharply raked wooden masts, the bluff-bowed schooner had been sailing the Great Lakes for nearly 18 years. Today's run was to pick up a load of lumber.

Two days out of Chicago and sailing without cargo, Captain Durnin paused to look over Green Bay's sparkling waters. He'd made good progress so far, but the wind had started to head the small schooner and, as he rounded to the north of Chambers Island, he figured he'd have to tack his way into the lumber port north of the city of Green Bay.

Oconto would be quiet and rural. The short, stocky skipper shook his head, wistfully. Not like bustling port of Chicago, with its newspapers that always got the latest news.

Captain Durnin had been following reports of the Civil War and President Abraham Lincoln's action to appoint Gen. Ulysses S. Grant to be Commander of all Union Forces. Maybe that'd turn

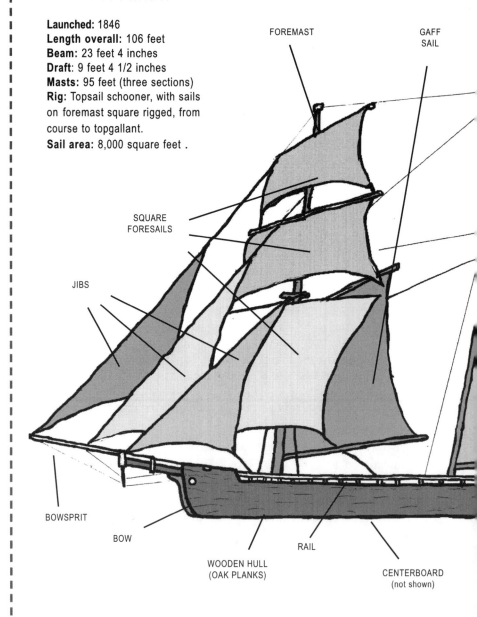

ALVIN CLARK

*Once the oldest wooden cargo vessel
on the Great Lakes*

Launched: 1846
Length overall: 106 feet
Beam: 23 feet 4 inches
Draft: 9 feet 4 1/2 inches
Masts: 95 feet (three sections)
Rig: Topsail schooner, with sails
on foremast square rigged, from
course to topgallant.
Sail area: 8,000 square feet .

FOREMAST

GAFF
SAIL

SQUARE
FORESAILS

JIBS

BOWSPRIT

BOW

RAIL

WOODEN HULL
(OAK PLANKS)

CENTERBOARD
(not shown)

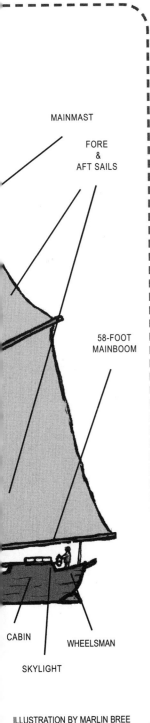

MAINMAST

FORE
&
AFT SAILS

58-FOOT
MAINBOOM

CABIN

WHEELSMAN

SKYLIGHT

ILLUSTRATION BY MARLIN BREE

the tide of battle, since the North was losing badly.

Because of the Civil War, good crewmembers were hard to find and the *Clark* had to sail out of Chicago shorthanded. Normally, she carried a captain, mate, cook, and four seamen — barely enough for a vessel of this size and complexity. But now she was manned only by the captain, a first mate, and a two-man crew, plus one passenger who was working his passage. She could not even rustle up a cook this sailing season.

One of the crew was a young Canadian from Toronto named Michael Cray, an able-bodied seaman who had already served one year in the Union Army. Onboard, he still wore his well-worn blue army tunic, but he had already served out his term of enlistment, so he was safe from the draft.

All were proud to be aboard the *Clark,* a 220-ton vessel, one of only 270 sailing vessels on all the Great Lakes. Launched in 1846, and built of white oak, she had an overall length of 106 feet, including her long bowsprit. Her masts were sharply raked, with her main mast soaring 95 feet above her deck.

Although a topsail schooner, she could be mistaken for a brigantine, since she had her three-piece foremast square rigged, from course to topgallant. This was so she could spread square sails before a following wind and scoot along on an easy run. In all, she could carry upwards of 8,000 square feet of sail.

Today she had her square rigged sails up, and, as they neared the northeast point of Chambers Island, Captain Durnin looked up once more to check to see how they were set.

Though they were sailing close hauled, he decided he'd keep up the square sails as long as they were pulling well. He'd have to watch them closely, because if the wind would come around some more, his reduced crew would have to go aloft to take in the sails. He also checked the set of the mainsail on its 58-foot boom. If that got caught aback, it could be a man-killer.

By late afternoon, a cloud formation had begun to build in the northeast. Captain Durnin studied the dark horizon with concern, for this was infamous Green Bay. He knew through his own experience that thunderstorms with extremely high winds could spring up suddenly and that in minutes the lake could develop towering waves. Like most experienced skippers, Captain Durnin had great respect for storms on Green Bay.

But the heavy weather appeared to be a passing rainstorm and there appeared to be no reason to shorten sail. After all, the *Clark* was making good time to the southwest. With luck, she'd make her port at the mouth of the Oconto River by nightfall.

WITHIN MINUTES, heavy clouds blacked out the horizon. On shore, a squall tore up trees by the roots and downed fences. Rain and hail reached the *Clark*, followed by high winds.

Putting the helm down, Captain Durnin shouted a warning to loosen the sheets. But as the *Clark* turned, her big sails caught the wind and filled bar taut. Slowly, the centerboard schooner rolled over on her starboard side and lay with water lapping at her rail.

Grabbing an ax, Crewman Cray managed to clambered forward on the steeply angled deck. The first gust passed and the *Clark* fought her way upright again. But with horror, Cray saw that the hatch covers were off. Only hours before, he and the crew had been down in the hold, sweeping it out to get ready for the next cargo.

There was no time to get the heavy wooden hatches back on.

Another, stronger gust slammed into the *Clark*, now turned dangerously broadside to the wind. The young crewman tried to loosen the foresheet, but it was under pressure and jammed. With his ax, he desperately began chopping at the sheets that held the sails trimmed for close-hauled sailing.

Too late. As the *Clark* went over, the young seaman threw down his ax and jumped to grab the windward rigging, his legs flying out from under him. In the driving rain and hail, he could only watch grimly as she rolled further down on her leeward side as chill waters roared into her open hatches.

A nearby vessel sent a yawl boat to pick up the survivors. Only Cray and another crewman were left alive.

The captain, the mate and the passenger were gone.

THE *CLARK* had filled with water through her open hatches and probably sank bow first, since she carried her steel anchors, pins and heavy chain forward. She slid to the bottom slowly and came to settle upright in the chill, dark depths. Her masts were still in her, projecting upward toward the light, with their tips only about 40 feet from the surface.

Over the years, she snuggled into the silt and cold fresh waters that would preserve her intact and undisturbed, lost to the outside world for more than 100 years.

IT WAS ON A RAW DAY in November 1967, when a commercial fisherman aboard the *Dellie W.*, out of Menominee, MI, cussed, threw his trawler into reverse and gave the powerful diesel the gun. But the nylon trawl net had become entangled in some unknown obstruction lying on the bottom off the northeast end of Chambers Island. After trying repeatedly to free it by pulling and maneuvering, Dick Garbowski cut the lead line and tied a buoy to the end, marking its location.

Disheartened by the loss of his valuable net, he returned ashore and called an amateur diver he knew to go down and take a look. Something had snagged it; maybe the diver, Frank Hoffmann, could untangle it and bring it back intact.

It was worth a try. Hoffmann was a diving enthusiast who ran a bar and motel in Egg Harbor, WI, on the Door County Peninsula. He'd been involved in some underwater searches and he also had an old boat he ran as a charter service for divers.

WITH THE AMATEUR DIVER ABOARD, the *Dellie W.* approached the markers where the nets had snagged. The day was bitter cold and windy, with temperatures in the 30s, and the waters were rough.

Captain Frank Hoffmann with one of the Clark's auxiliary anchors

On the way out, the fishermen for the first time told Hoffmann that they had made a sonar scan of the bottom area and their readings showed a ship down there. It probably was an old one, since they saw masts, but they didn't much care: they wanted their $1,400 net back.

Shivering in the cold, Hoffmann donned his wet suit, pulled on his double SCUBA tanks, flippers, and grabbed his old diving light, which sometimes didn't work. He also tied on two knives (one to use; one to lose), in case of trouble. Nets can be dangerous entanglements to divers and for safety, SCUBA divers usually go down in pairs. But on such a short notice, Hoffmann couldn't get anyone to dive with him.

Jumping off the fishing boat, the lone diver dove to follow the lead line down. In the murky water roiled by late fall waves, he was not surprised that visibility was poor. At about 50 feet down, he switched on his diving light, but he could see only six feet ahead. At 90 feet, something loomed large in the darkness. He couldn't see much in his feeble yellow light, but he soon realized that he was looking at the undamaged front end of an old ship – a very old wooden ship.

His battered diving lamp began to blink. He shook it, and in its wavering illumination, he moved slowly forward. Time to go to work.He could see the net wrapped around the bow in several places. Reaching for his diving knife, he found he had lost it, so he pulled out his spare. But as he worked one line free, he found that another section of net also had to be cut.

As he grabbed the net, his diving light went out. In the bottom's blackness, he yanked on the net and found himself bouncing up and down – surface waves were jousting with the net's buoys. To his amazement, the jiggling turned his light back on and he saw that the nets were extensively tangled in a number of places and he knew couldn't free the nets in a single dive.

He glanced at his diving watch: his bottom time was up and he made his way to the surface, watching the water grow brighter as he arose out of the chill depths. By the time the *Dellie W.'s* crew hoisted him aboard, he was shivering uncontrollably.

But he was filled with excitement. He had not retrieved their net, but he had located what looked like every diver's dream – a virgin shipwreck.

WHEN HE RETURNED TO HIS BAR, Hoffmann called friends who were amateur SCUBA divers. Before he moved to Egg Harbor, Hoffmann had run a janitorial service in Chicago and was an active sport diver. His friends headed to Door County the following weekend, wondering what he had found.

He had only been down on the bottom a few minutes, in limited visibility, but he had done it again: found another wreck.

Moreover, the wreck was technically his. The fishermen didn't have an interest in an old ship; they mostly just wanted their valuable net, so Hoffmann worked out a deal so that the net and any salvageable cargo aboard would go to the fishermen.

But the ship would belong to Hoffmann.

Even so, Hoffmann's friends hoped it was not a repeat of the *Jennybel*. A few years back, a commercial fishing boat had wrapped its nets around an old vessel that also had sunk on stormy Green Bay. She turned out to be an old schooner, lying upright in about 95 feet of water, beside a deep trench. She had sunk in 1881 while being towed from Death's Door following a capsizing accident and was still filled with cordwood. Once again, local fishermen had snagged their valuable nets and they wanted the nets cleared and brought up. Diving on the schooner, Hoffmann had cleared the nets for the fishermen but later had talked in public about raising her. She was, he boasted, a very old schooner sitting upright with her hull intact and her masts still standing. Nobody had found an intact schooner like this before.

People were fascinated with his tale, especially rival divers, who made secret night dives on her, took off some artifacts and one night actually attempted to raise her. When Hoffmann heard about it, he raced out in his boat and screamed at the amateur salvagers to stop. They had towed a barge out atop the old schooner, fastened a single, heavy cable around the ship's bow and another around her stern, and joined these two looped cables at a single, central union. But as the crane continued to lift, the old schooner broke in half – her hull snapped like a twig.

The broken old boat is still down on the bottom, stripped of anything of interest or value. Hoffmann had lost his schooner – but learned a valuable lesson.

This time, Hoffmann swore everyone to secrecy. Once again, he was concerned that other amateur divers might come in and loot the wreck for souvenirs or even try to raise her.

It was a free-for-all time in the 1960s when there were no archeological laws in place to protect historic wrecks. Anyone could go down on a sunken vessel and "souvenir" it to bare bones.

It would be Hoffmann's wreck – so long as no one else knew about it.

IT WAS A CHILL AND WINDY November 6 when the Garbowski trawler *Dellie W.* again headed out for the wreck site. Onboard were Hoffmann and several fellow divers to do a survey of the old boat and also to free the net that was tangled in several places on the old schooner.

With Hoffmann were Dick Boyd and his diving partner, Carl Poster, both from Madison. Hoffmann had already been down on an exploratory dive with Bud Brain, of Chicago, but had spent only a little bottom time on the wreck.

As Boyd and Poster descended, they were surprised by the poor visibility of only three to four feet and by 50 feet of depth, all surface light was erased. The divers could only see what their dive lights illuminated – a small pattern that penetrated a few feet into the black water.

"We saw nothing until we hit the deck at about 90 feet," Boyd recalled. Onboard the old vessel, he began to feel a chill coming over him. He knew what was happening: At that depth, his wet suit of foam neoprene had compressed to one-fourth of its original thickness, losing much of its insulating value as well as its positive buoyancy.

He shrugged it off, entranced by what he saw. "We could instantly sense that the wooden vessel was in remarkable condition," he said. Leaving the descending line, the sport divers followed the rail toward the stern of the ship. The deck inside the rail was littered with blocks, pulleys, and other sailing artifacts.

"Some distance back, peering inward toward the ship's midline," Boyd related, "we could make out a giant, post-like object projecting into the gloom...it slowly dawned on us that a mast was still standing. The realization that we were exploring a totally intact sailing schooner complete with standing masts finally crystallized in our chilled brains."

When they swam over several cargo holds, they saw that the hatch covers were missing.

Reaching the aft cabin, they peered in the companionway to see that the cabin was completely silted in. They could not get a good look at the entire boat because, at a depth of up to 110 feet, they were working in blackness penetrated only about six feet by the lights of their diving lamps. Their movements would stir up bottom silt, cutting what little visibility they had even more.

Checking the fishing net, the divers saw that it was wrapped in many places around the schooner's windlass, the forward bit post and the mast pin rail. They began to make plans to free the net without cutting it, but concluded that it would take a number of dives to free the entanglement.

When their 15 minutes of bottom time were up, they ascended the line, taking a short safety decompression stop at 10 feet. Back aboard the fishing trawler, the divers were jubilant. They had been on a schooner of exceptional interest, completely intact with both masts still standing.

She was a virgin wreck, but a boat of mystery.

Who was she? How old was she? They had not seen a name board or other form of identification, nor for that matter, had they found any clue as to her actual age.

But she clearly was very old.

NOVEMBER WINDS SCOURED the lake, kicking up big waves. Secured to a dock in Egg Harbor, with no shelter from the pounding waves and wind, the 50-ton Garbowski trawler *Dellie W.* broke loose from her mooring lines and ran aground.

Diver Bernie Bloom recalls Hoffmann "running around like a crazy man," trying to make a rescue effort. "Frank tried to take his small boat out to pull the *Dellie W.* off the beach. The engine roared, the boat took up the strain, but the only thing Hoffman did was tear the Sampson post off his boat."

The *Dellie W.* rolled over on her side with her bottom to the sea and her starboard deck down in the water. Waves thundered against her thick steel hull and she pounded against the bottom.

Finally, it took three big diesel-powered fishing trawlers to drag the *Dellie W.* free. The big trawler was damaged and it would take time to get repairs and return her to service.

The divers were out of luck.

HOFFMANN COULDN'T WAIT for the trawler to get repaired, so he decided to take his 27-foot powerboat, *Sea Witch*, to the dive site. But as Bernie Bloom recalls, "she was a wooden junker that had tin covering her bottom. She leaked heavily."

It was a ride to the dive site he'd always remember. "As we motored out, the weather was cold, foggy and nasty."

It was late in the diving season and they planned to make two dives. On the first dive, they worked to clear the net, but without a lot of success. They found that the net under full trawl was wound around the bow section and snagged hard into the bowsprit, anchors and catheads.

"It was a downright treacherous job," Boyd recalled. "As the trawler had initially attempted to pull the net free, the net had become stretched across the ship's bow and her forward fixtures. Taut as a banjo strings, they had to be cut carefully free by the divers." When entangled lines and mesh were severed, they could whip outward or upward with great force – and the result could be deadly.

After they spent 15 minutes on the bottom, they ascended to end their first dive session.

The divers had to wait out their full decompression time before doing their second dive, so they decided to boat over to Menominee for lunch. They dropped off one diver to return to his home.

As they motored back to the dive site, the temperature had dropped to just above freezing. By 4 p.m., it was growing dark and they couldn't find their markers.

"By this time it was blustery and snowing," Bloom recalls. The infamous Gales of November had descended.

As the light faded, they had about given up when Bloom saw the marker bobbing in the chill waves. "I secretly thought of keeping my mouth shut," he said.

Instead, he called out, "Here it is."

After they tied off their boat to the marker, they got into their cold, wet diving suits and all three, Hoffman, Bud Brain and Bloom, went down in their SCUBA gear.

"It was a dumb thing to do, to leave the boat unattended," Bloom later recalled. "But we were in a state of high excitement."

In the darkness pierced by their dive lights, they descended the line mostly by feel and then followed the mast down.

"Fear was something you got used to," Bernie Bloom said.

"You went down, down in the dark, and you couldn't see anything. *Bang!* You get a little adrenaline jolt as you see something in front of you. You reach out and touch it: your ship. You were home."

Photo / Dick Boyd

Divers inspect the century-old, leather covered rope still attached to a wooden block salvaged from the Clark. Frank Hoffman (right) holds the block as divers Jack Raymond (left) and Dick Boyd (right) look on.

IN THE FLICKERING LIGHT OF THEIR LAMPS, they leveled out a few feet above the deck and began moving to the cabin. "Swim fast and you run right into it," Bloom recalled, "because you can only see a few feet." He added, "But you get used to it."

A loose plank to the cabin's portside was hanging loose and the young diver pulled it free. Peering inside, he could see the ship's galley and nearby, a pestle, a wooden board, and a hunk of soap, still intact. Bloom grabbed the soap as a souvenir.

Exploring some more, they swam over the stern to look for a name board, but couldn't find any identification. The ship was still a mystery.

When their bottom time was up, they swam back to the mainmast and ascended. At its tip, they found the line to their marker buoy and went up to the surface. By the time they poked their heads above water, the waves were growing. Their boat was still there, faithfully bobbing with its nose to the storm.

"It was a hell of a ride back, dark and snowing," Bloom recalled. "And if our compass had gone out, we'd still be out there circling."

They hadn't bothered to get out of their wet suits and they

were chilled to the bone. Bloom recalled sleeping in front of a fireplace, but never getting warm and in some stage of hypothermia.

"But we did a lot of that in those days," he said.

The diving season was definitely over for the year.

O VER THE WINTER, Hoffmann obtained official salvage rights to the old vessel. He alone owned it legally, and, he vowed to protect it from marauding amateur divers who, he feared, would "souvenir" bare the unprotected vessel.

His amateur diving group, enraptured by the lost schooner, was composed of divers from Chicago, Green Bay, and around southern Illinois and central Wisconsin. All drove over to spend time diving. They paid their own expenses and worked for free.

Hoffman paid for equipment and the operation of his leaky old boats, no mean feat for a small-time saloonkeeper. But costs were mounting. Hoffmann had discovered an underwater archeological treasure, but he was facing a personal financial disaster.

In winter meetings, the divers began to plan what they wanted to do with the sunken boat. Everyone wanted to "keep it all intact, and not strip it."

It was the dream every diver hoped for: a virgin wreck undamaged and untouched, and looking as if she could sail away on her own bottom. They felt privileged to be able to dive on a pristine vessel and they were in awe of her.

They were lucky, too. She was preserved because she had gone down in fresh water. Old ships in salt water don't last long underwater because their metal fittings rust away, their wood is devoured by wood-eating worms, and the ships collapse inward upon themselves, often in little more than a half-century. But in fresh water depths, the cold and the lack of salt and oxygen allow boats to remain relatively undamaged for long periods of time.

Whoever she was, she was a unique old boat, all right, and beautiful. She had captured their imaginations and their hearts.

They were determined to salvage her, somehow.

T HE NEXT SPRING, as soon as the ice was off Green Bay, the divers went out to their dive site and, confounded, looked around for their buoys. They were missing.

Storms over the winter had blown away their markers. They had lost her.

Undaunted, they spent days relocating the wreck and put in new and more substantial markers. Sliding down the lines, the divers probed the wreck. They were amazed to find that the hull seemed solid and remarkably well preserved. It was intact, except for some of the booms and rigging that were missing, but the divers figured they had to be around somewhere in the silt. The cargo holds, open to view, were filled with mud.

The divers discovered that the ship's wheel had a curious fabric covering on it. When they touched it, the canvas covering over the spokes disintegrated. They decided the heavy cloth was a safety measure to keep a helmsman from breaking an arm or a wrist in the wheel's spokes during heavy weather.

Diving was complicated because, as the divers swam around in darkness, their movements stirred up bottom silt. Visibility was so poor, Hoffmann said, "we could hold a diving light against our face masks and barely make out the dim glow of the filament inside."

They decided that they needed some kind of suction device to clean out the silt inside the cabin and the holds. Because the amateur group of divers had no funds to buy this equipment, they began experimenting with various makeshift systems they could put together.

Early efforts only roiled up the silt.

After they burned up several small pumps, they hadn't even cleared out the small cabin. They needed a bigger device and Hoffmann scrounged up an old five-inch fire pump, which had been used by the village of Egg Harbor. They'd gotten it as Army Surplus.

With a bigger pump, they needed a bigger boat.

Hoffmann's two small wooden boats wouldn't do, since they often were dangerously overloaded with crew, pumps, diving gear and equipment. Moreover, Hoffmann's 27-foot *Sea Witch* and 34-foot *Sea Ranger* were old and leaky.

The divers called them three-man boats:

One to pilot, one to keep the machinery running, and one to bail.

They weren't kidding.

HAROLD DERUSHA, of Marinette Marine Corp., had been following the amateur divers' problems. Finally, he decided to
step in: "Come and get the barge," he said.

Everyone was amazed.

Derusha had just offered the divers the loan of his World War
II-era landing craft, *Cleo's Barge*, a 56-foot vessel that would
hold the big new pump and its engine.

"It had twin diesels. A cabin. It was big," Bloom said enthusiastically. "And best of all, it had *heat*."

Moreover, Derusha told them that when they needed diesel
fuel, just to stop by his business and fill up. It was an incredible
offer. The amateur divers now had a big craft and all the fuel they
wanted.

But after they mounted their fire pump on *Cleo's Barge,* they
had to figure out how to get their giant suction device working to
clear out more than a century of silt and mud from the vessel. The
job was enormous: they had to move 20,000 cubic feet of mud.

Ingeniously, they tied an aluminum pipe to the sunken
schooner's upright mast. To this they attached flexible hoses, at
the top to *Cleo,* and at the bottom, to the divers. When *Cleo* left
the diving site for the night, they could disconnect the flexible
tube and leave the underwater gear in place, ready to hook up the
next day. Below, the divers would be ready to pick up their flexible hose from where they left it the day before. It was a good
system.

They added two screens, one at the intake on the wreck and
another at the surface. That way they wouldn't lose any artifact
that might get sucked up.

To work the new suction device, one diver remained at the bottom, moving the intake over the silt to suck it up. In the close
confines of the cabin or the hold, only one diver could work at a
time. He labored alone in silt and blackness, often losing his
sense of direction.

It was hard, mean work, and a challenge for the bravest of
divers.

"You went into the hold," Bloom recalls, "and wrapped your
legs around the pipe." The diver held the suction head between
his legs and leaned out, scooping mud with both arms toward the
wire screen at the end of the hose.

Diver Dick Boyd surfaces with a porcelain bowl retrieved from the ship's galley. Later, the bowl was dated by markings to 1862, giving the first clue to the age of the Mystery Ship. Life expectancy of glassware aboard sailing vessels was very short.

When the divers were scooping in the cabin's darkness, they could only feel the artifacts as they came toward the power head. They picked these out and set them outside on the deck, only a couple of feet away.

Divers faced several dangers. One was the possibility that the excavation might collapse over them like an underwater grave, leaving them alone and trapped under tons of mud. With silt and debris billowing about, there was also possibility that a diver's regulator might clog up. Or, the big suction hose might tear out of his grasp, flogging back and forth and injuring the diver. It took steely nerves.

Like most divers, Bloom shrugged off the dangers: "I once encountered a mudslide," he said, "because the tool and I inadvertently dug a tunnel that gently collapsed on me."

But that didn't prevent him from continuing. "The water with the mud kept the mud fluid and not in a dangerous situation," he said. "You just dug your way back out."

They began turning their diving lights off. "It saved the battery, and, besides it was so dark you couldn't see anything anyway," Bloom recalled.

The amateur divers were making their own underwater lights by wiring an automotive sealed-beam spotlight ("good to 200 feet") to a battery and stuffing that in a fiberglass case.

Here the divers divided into two distinct technology camps:

Some preferred to hang their underwater lamps with straps to their wrists. Others fastened them to a hockey helmet so that wherever their head turned, they'd have light.

The extreme depths and the chill 30- to 40-degree waters at the bottom took their toll. Their foam-neoprene suits in these depths compressed, taking away part of the suit's normal heat-retaining insulation and making the divers chill. The divers learned to work in 20-minute shifts. They found that 20 minutes on the bottom would allow them to surface without having to decompress in stages as they ascended.

Even so, divers often came up shivering from the bottom cold.

IT TOOK A MONUMENTAL AMOUNT OF WORK to clear out the cabin and after that, the forepeak and the holds. The divers removed an estimated 10 tons of mud and silt from inside the old vessel. Up came artifacts including plates, dishes, silverware, some leather items and tools.

From the silted galley, they recovered several porcelain China pieces. Emblems on the bottoms dated them back to the early 1860s, indicating that the vessel was probably pre-Civil War.

"This discovery," Dick Boyd recalls, "generated great public and media interest and was the catalyst for the intense media scrutiny that then began to follow the project."

In addition to the China, the divers found some remarkable artifacts. "In one case, a duck with its flesh still in place was found within the silt," Boyd said. "This bird was a deep-diving species so we assumed that it simply had gotten trapped within the hull long after it sank. Upon closer inspection, it became apparent that the creature's head had been cut off and its feathers had been plucked and singed. In short, it had been prepared for cooking."

The frigid environment had preserved its flesh intact for 105 years.

At about the time the discoveries were being made, the divers made a tentative identification of the boat they were diving on and learned about the loss of life during the *Alvin Clark*'s sinking. Three victims had never been recovered.

"After seeing the preserved, fleshy duck," Boyd recalls, "the divers working inside the ship in total darkness became very anxious whenever they encountered any soft, spongy mass."

The divers discovered another unique artifact: a simple earthenware jar of homemade cheese. It was common foodstuff aboard sailing vessels and it was called "crock cheese."

When the silt was removed, Boyd reported, "the cheese proved to be unspoiled and edible." When the cheese later was examined at the University of Wisconsin, the bacterium used to produce the curd was still recoverable in a viable state. Shortly after they brought it up, several adventurous divers tasted a tiny bit of the cheese from this large crock.

"To say the least, it wasn't very good," Boyd said. "However, I'm told that sailor's crock cheese was pretty bad even when it was freshly made."

They sent this cheese to the Kraft's Food Museum in Philadelphia, where it resides in all its glory as the world's oldest edible cheese – another marvel from the Mystery Ship.

F INANCIALLY, THEY WERE BARELY SCRAPING BY. Hoffmann joked that their diving work was patched together by Christian Brothers' brandy and carpet tape.

The brandy was for the divers coming up from the chilled waters and the carpet tape was to tape up holes in the divers' suits. It also patched other things, including holes in the flexible suction tubes.

Undaunted, they decided to try to raise the *Clark*.

On September 24, 1968, they began boring underneath the wreck. They decided that her hull was in good enough shape to raise and besides, they'd excavated most of the mud from inside of the ship. Now all they had to do was bore a small hole through the mud all the way under the vessel and out the other side.

They ingeniously found a way to reverse the engine and use the former suction head as a power blower with 200 pounds of pressure. Marinette Marine built them a special water jet cutting head: an inch-and-a-half diameter pipe with a curved radius, with side pressure vents to neutralize the blast.

The plan was to insert the water jet head down into the clay and silt to follow the hull's curvature, but they found the unit had a lot of back pressure. Bloom said the unit moved him around underwater, so they solved their problem by getting their biggest diver, Gary Means, to wrestle the cutting tool. That worked.

Figuring out how to get the holes straight was a special problem. Means would go to his diving station, marked out ahead of time, and Bloom would swim straight out over the deck. When he could see Means' light, he'd cut 90 degrees to the ship's keel.

The big engine on *Cleo* threw 200 pounds of pressure into the water jet. Means shoved it into the mud and it dug like crazy until it popped out on the other side – "like a blowtorch through butter," Bloom said. They put a line on the head, and when they pulled it back out – they had a line under the keel.

"It worked beautiful," Bloom said.

Late in the season, the lake was acting up with large swells. Snow was on the way. Several times they had to postpone dives because the barge was moving so much that it tossed the hose about, making it impossible for the divers to work. In all, they dug seven holes – one twice, because it got crooked

The weather was freezing and waves were running up to five feet. But they had few days left and divers went down to attach lifting cables to the under-hull slings. They did one or two at a time, leaving the cables fall back to the deck after they were finished, awaiting a final hookup.

They removed everything from the hull that would interfere with her raising, including anchors, loose chain and fittings. They also brought up more artifacts, including the captain's writing desk, a brass locket, clay pipes, a clock, an oil lamp, and a wallet.

The wreck was ready for lifting.

MONEY WAS RUNNING OUT. Hoffmann had borrowed heavily and these funds were used up. Over the winter, Hoffmann tried unsuccessfully to launch a fund raising. Though the diving group got great publicity, very little cash was coming in. Marinette Marine contributed some money.

Hoffmann took out a second mortgage on his bar and motel. He bought gear and supplies on his credit cards.

Privately, he hoped for financial success when and if the *Clark* could be raised. It would be a one-of-a- kind vessel, brought back from the deep, a sure-fire tourist attraction.

In reality he was slowly going broke.

The strain began to show. Originally, he intended to bring the *Clark* to Door County, where the beautiful area's booming tourist trade might provide a base for financial support.

After a series of combative disagreements, Hoffmann turned his back on the tourism-rich peninsula where he had his bar and looked instead to the opposite side of Green Bay. Though the tourist trade was thinner on this side of the lake – much, much thinner – Hoffmann still hoped that his fantastic find could be put on display to pay its own way. If he put it up, they would come.

It was to become a major strategic error on his part.

In June 1969, the diving season opened with winds blowing so hard that the *Cleo's* anchor line snapped and the divers had to return to shore.

The next day, they successfully anchored over the wreck and started pumping silt again. The amateur divers began to collect any artifacts that had fallen around the wreck site and to get the old schooner ready to be raised. That meant removing the masts.

"But who the hell knew how to take the masts out of a hundred year old boat?" Bloom recalled. "They sit in a hole in the keel, and wedged into the deck, with the wedges tapering in both directions."

He added appreciatively, "A beautiful fit. And swelled in after being down that long."

They quickly ran into trouble. Their first attempt was to pry out the wedges from the topside deck, but they couldn't budge the water-swollen wood. Next, they went below into the hold and tried to push the wedges up from the underside. The result was that they broke two jacks, each with a five-ton capacity.

Undaunted, they built a special jack atop an adjustable base made by placing three pipes with successively decreasing diameter inside each other. This formed an enormously strong pedestal, atop which they mounted a ten-ton hydraulic ram. It took two divers to take this device below decks, place the base against the ship's keel, and jack up the ram to push the wedges up and out.

All the work was done in the confined, silty darkness of the hold. It was, as Boyd later recalled, "a truly daunting endeavor." But it worked.

Once they got the wedges out, they still had to figure out how to raise the masts.

And how, exactly, to raise the 220-ton schooner. It seemed almost an impossible task.

They first considered air bags, but the divers soon discarded the concept since they needed to control the rate of ascent. Once the hull broke loose from the bottom, the air bags could come up too fast, possibly injuring a diver. Or their velocity from 110 feet could be too uneven or too great, allowing the schooner to wobble, break out of the slings, or even to damage surface vessels.

Finally, they decided to use old-fashioned hand-powered winches to mechanically raise the old boat at the rate they wanted and with great control.

Marionette Marine donated a lift barge to be anchored in place atop the *Clark*. On each side of the barge, workers welded powerful, if cumbersome, hand-powered winches. Bloom recalls: "Jim DeRusha, son of the owner of Marinette Marine and a Naval Architect, told us what and how to do it."

To get ready for the lift, they first had to raise the masts. Divers went down to the old schooner and tied loops of line around each mast.

A crane mounted on a Gallagher Marine Construction Barge took up the strain, diesel engine roaring, and up came the old masts without any problem.

After being underwater for more than 105 years, the masts were in excellent condition. It was a good omen.

By 4 a.m. Wednesday, July 23, they were ready to raise the *Clark*. It was dark on the water, with a slight chill in the air in the pre-dawn hours.

They decided to go ahead, rather than wait. Since the divers were working in darkness anyway on the bottom, there was no reason to hold off the long-awaited project for daylight hours.

The hull was sitting in about 10 feet of mud, so divers went down and began sluicing mud from the low side of the hull with the water jet. Other divers fitted slings to the lifting cables.

They began cranking the hand-powered winches on the *Clark's* low side, canted to starboard.

After a century of submersion, the intact Alvin Clark *surfaces at Marinette Marine Corp before an estimated 20,000 excited onlookers. Note her wheel and doghouse.*

THE BARGE SQUATTED DOWN in the water about 8 inches. They watched, expectantly, worried about the strain, but the cables held. Twelve men cranked harder and the barge sank another four inches. Suddenly, it bobbed up six inches.

"The rolling action broke the suction on the bottom," Bloom said. The wreck was free of the mud and suspended beneath the barges in her slings.

But it took 100 turns on a single winch to raise the wreck 5 inches. A crew could last only about 100 turns on a single winch, they discovered, before another crew had to take over the job.

Boaters who came out for a look at the salvage operation were invited on board and they also were persuaded to take a turn at the four winches. "We exhausted everyone who came along," Bloom said.

The cumbersome hand-powered winches were slow, but they gave the divers total control of their lift.

By 3 p.m., the wreck was within 60 feet of the surface. A storm approached, and the crew took up the barge's anchors and began moving the boat toward shore.

At the same time, volunteers cranked frantically to raise the *Clark* – they didn't want to lose her now.

The squall hit with high winds and heavy rain, but dissipated in about half an hour. The schooner had stayed in place.

As they moved toward shore, the *Clark* dragged bottom in about 45 feet of water, and, the day's effort was over. *Cleo's Barge* set her anchors. The divers were exhausted.

They had worked nearly nonstop for two days.

THE NEXT DAY, they brought her up river to Marinette Marine. All during the trip, the divers continued cranking the ship up, watching expectantly. There was a stirring in the water. Finally, ahead of the barge, the schooner's bowsprit broke water – the first time in 105 years that the old schooner had come back to the surface.

Crowds lining the river's banks cheered lustily. The divers were jubilant, clapping each other on the back.

At Marinette Marine, two large cranes on barges and two on shore took over the job and continued to lift the old vessel. She broke surface, decks awash but still intact. Pumps whirred to drive water out; the divers clambered aboard and enthusiastically grabbed buckets to remove the last of the bottom mud inside her.

It was a joyous, momentous, and historic moment. The effort had taken two years and approximately 3,000 dives.

The *Alvin Clark* was afloat again.

Never before had a vessel like this, in mint condition and floating on her own, been reclaimed intact from the deep.

Hoffmann and his crew stood in open-eyed admiration. Though he and his divers had been diving for years in the dark depths, they now saw for the first time the entire ship.

"We were amazed as much as anyone else," he said.

They had another surprise: the *Clark* floated on her own bottom. Once she was pumped out, she floated beautifully and the shipyard took the pumps out.

The divers discovered her seams were still tight and her caulking still in place after more than a century underwater.

The Clark's bow section (left) shows remarkable shipwright work, including square-headed nails on planks. About one hour after dewatering, the cranes slacked off and the vessel floated on her own after 105 years of submersion. The deck cabin (below) came up largely intact. The topmost structure is a skylight.

All Photos/
Dick Boyd

Inside the hull (above), the planking was discovered to be remarkably tight. At right is the centerboard trunk. View is looking toward the stern. The entire area held at least six feet of compacted silt when the vessel was discovered. Below, diver Bob Olmstead inspects the vessel's wheel. Trays in background atop the cabin hold artifacts which had been sorted and cataloged from various parts of the ship.

Photo / Dick Boyd

After a year of controlled kiln drying to minimize wood cracking and deterioration, the Alvin Clark floats on the Menominee River in 1970 at the Mystery Ship Seaport Museum. Her rigging is largely restored, including the 58-foot boom.

S HE WAS REFERRED TO as the "Mystery Ship," or, "The Mystery Ship from 19 Fathoms." The latter was Hoffmann's imaginative invention.

But before she was brought to the surface, researchers had been trying to identify her through old newspaper accounts and government records.

Their detective work led them to put together certain facts: a vessel by the name of the *Clark* was known to have sunk under storm conditions with loss of life in the location in which the *Mystery Ship* was found.

The *Clark* was 110 feet LOA; the Mystery Ship was the same length. The boat was built in 1846 – about the age of the boat on the bottom.

They were pretty sure it was the *Clark,* but there was no trail board or name on her hull for a certain identification.

The clincher came when divers found a stencil on a trunk onboard that was attributed to Michael Cray, of Toronto, one of the two crewmembers that survived the sinking.

She was positively identified.

However, not a lot could be found about the first few years of the *Clark.* "Most records suggest that she went to work in the salt trade on the eastern lakes," Boyd said.

In 1856, William Higgie, of Racine, Wisconsin, purchased her. The Higgie boys were essentially timber transporters for several prominent Michigan "timber barons."

Boyd added, "It was well known that many of these 'barons' poached trees off lands belonging to the Federal Government. Once this contraband wood entered the Chicago Timber Market, it became virtually untraceable – a very profitable venture with only minor risks."

"The *Clark* was indeed used to run poached lumber down Lake Michigan to Chicago," he said. "There are several interesting reports of federal timber marshals pursuing the *Clark* and attempting to arrest her master for theft of government property. Even though several arrests were made, the federal agents were never able to make any official charges stick."

He concluded: "It could be said that the *Clark* was a sort of early 'pirate ship' on the Great Lakes before the Civil War."

F LAGS FLYING, the *Clark* was towed proudly to Menominee, where she was put on display during the annual Blessing of the Watercraft ceremony. About 30,000 people gazed in awe at the old ship, floating on her own bottom, masts proudly lifted to the heavens.

During the winter of 1969 – 1970, she was placed in an enclosure and a makeshift dry kiln began to slowly dry her out. She emerged intact and was cleaned up and brought to her new home, the Mystery Ship Seaport, in a land-based slip specially designed for her in Menominee.

She was to be a museum attraction, hopefully attracting thousands who had seen the news of her miraculous rising from the depths.

Those who saw her marveled: she looked a lot like when she went down, only with her wood silvered and gray. The noted naval historian, Howard Chapelle, of the Smithsonian Institution, Washington, D.C., wrote to Hoffman:

"This is a true treasure of the Great Lakes. Your recovery of the schooner is of far greater importance than a few gold coins or a hull fragment of a supposed treasure ship. In your find we will now be able to put together in great part the real working craft of the past."

"You got her up, Frank," someone said, adding, "Now what are you doing to do with her?"

It was a good question.

EPILOGUE

THE *CLARK* RESTED IN HER DRYDOCK CRADLE, but the crowds quickly dwindled. The funds generated by the museum were not enough to care for her. Without so much as the protection of a new coat of paint or wood preservative, she sat uncovered through season after season, open to rain, frost, snow and the heat of summer.

Slowly, she began to decay.

When I made my visit to the *Clark* about 12 years later, she was a vessel in distress. Her wood planking was gray and silvery; black in some places. The firm hull had begun to hog and I could see substantial sagging.

As I stepped aboard, I sensed trouble. Beneath my feet, the wood in places seemed springy. In fact, spongy.

I tried to focus on the boat itself, this magnificent old wind machine brought back from the depths. I walked the deck to the aft mast, trying to imagine what it was like to try to control this huge craft in any sort of wind. Just looking at the masts sticking up nearly 100 feet gave me a sense of awe and new appreciation for the sailors in these old schooners.

I especially noted the 58-foot boom, so large it overhung the aft section of the boat. How would one hank on sail or manage this huge mass of canvas in a blow?

Gingerly, I ducked my head to enter the aft cabin. It was large, as befits an ancient lake schooner, nearly 14 feet long and taking up the full breadth of the hull. It was bright in here and I saw a hole where a raised skylight would have been.

But as I eased myself inside, my foot went down – I had almost stuck my shoe through the rotten flooring. I backed out warily.

In the hold, she seemed sound enough. I noted with a shiver of dread that the large wooden case adjacent to her keel meant she was a center boarder. My own sailboat was a centerboard boat – no permanent outside keel with weight.

That was what had killed her.

In a blast of wind, she lay over on her side, and without a lead mine of ballast below, she could not climb back up and right herself. I tried not to analyze her last moments as she wallowed in the storm, her hatches above me letting in torrents of water, all flooding below.

Slowly, the hull must have filled up. Right where I was standing.

I scampered up a notched pole that served as a ladder up to the weather deck. Sighting down her massive hull, I could see that she had badly hogged – her hull had warped. This was not what I had expected from all the publicity she had been given.

When I met Hoffmann, he seemed undaunted. "A little money and she'll sail again," he told me.

I was not at all certain. She looked far too gone.

I must have showed my skepticism in my face. He added, "Oh, it'll take a little work, but underneath she's as sound as she can be."

He wandered off. I looked around: on this fine weekend day, there was only a handful of visitors.

As a tourist attraction, she was a bust. There was not enough money coming in to cover the costs of raising her, much less to pay for her preservation.

Hoffmann, saddled with debt and his love of the old ship, turned everywhere for help, but met only failure. The *Clark* was too big to move on land, too rotted to put to sea, and no museum felt it had the resources to take on a project the size of the *Clark*. She was like a beached whale.

Hoffman and his volunteers had brought back this treasure from the depths at great sacrifice, with great courage and great persistence, and she was rotting away. He could not take care of her and he could not let her go. He could not get the help he wanted from others, either. He began to drink heavily.

There was also the question of jurisdiction. Was she raised in Wisconsin waters – or Michigan's? That would give one or the other state some legal claim to her, but she lay so close to the state line that inevitable wrangling occurred.

A fire broke out aboard. The report I heard was that a drunken Hoffmann, demented by his sad state of affairs, had tried to torch his own boat. Later reports said that Hoffmann had simply knocked a kerosene lantern over on deck and the small fire was quickly put out.

An increasingly desperate Hoffmann offered to sell his beloved ship to the city of Menominee, but they turned him down.

He tried to sell her to other municipalities and ports throughout the Great Lakes, also without success.

TOWARD THE END, the *Clark* herself simply gave up. She flattened down, caving inward, after her fastenings rusted through. Her keel cracked, and the vessel settled on her side. She was a disintegrating shambles of what she was when she was brought to the surface – the oldest and most significant wreck ever discovered on the Lakes.

Though she was given a State Historical Site designation, the *Clark* became the object of worldwide historical and naval archeological horror – a chilling and heart-rending example what not to do when divers find a shipwreck.

In her wake she left a broken Hoffmann.

In 1987, he finally sold the *Clark*, and more importantly, the land on which she rested to local investors. The waterfront property had increasingly become prime real estate and in 1994 operators brought in a bulldozer.

The *Clark's* rotted timbers were no match for the heavy machine and she was broken up quickly, shoved aside by the blade, and ground down under the heavy tracks. Big chunks of what was left were carted off and burned. But part of her still lies under the asphalt of a parking lot.

Hoffman fled south to live with his eroded dreams in a trailer park in Florida. Those who knew him say he talked sadly of the *Clark* until his death some years later.

If there was anything that came out of the tragedy, it was a study of what goes wrong when old boats are recovered and brought to the surface.

In 1987, the federal government enacted the Abandoned Shipwrecks act, which regulates underwater archeology sites, claiming that an abandoned ship is the property of the state in which it lies. Divers may not remove any property, under penalty of law, nor may they raise the ship. The legislation was drafted after the sad experience of the *Alvin Clark.* In 1988, Wisconsin enacted funding for the State Underwater Archeology Program.

Bernie Bloom sums it all up this way: "Frank was in over his head. It was all very difficult, and Frank had an alcoholic problem. Worse, he did not have the touch."

As other historic ships came in line for federal funding, such as San Diego's *Star of India*, and received infusions of money, the *Clark* was bypassed. Never able to secure any grants for protection of his beloved schooner and ignored by legislators and representatives, Hoffman became incensed.

His problems grew as did his drinking.

The technology for saving old ships was not fully developed. Ships raised over the years, such as the *Vasa* in Sweden or the *Mary Rose* in England, had specially designed, humidity-controlled buildings erected over them and they were sprayed continuously with chemical preservatives.

They were not left out in the weather, as the old schooner was.

Bloom says, "In 20 years, there was zero real maintenance on it."

"It was a noble effort," he related, with a sigh, "and today not given its due. We hear comments that we should not have raised it. And once we raised it, we didn't do anything with it."

He paused a moment. "These days, I am pugnacious on this point: We had the ship. But where were all the experts when we needed them?"

For further information on the Alvin Clark,
please refer to Author's Notes.

FOUR

THE

LAST RACE

OF THE

EDMUND FITZGERALD

Propeller churning, the Edmund Fitzgerald *heads out of the Duluth-Superior harbor onto the open waters of Lake Superior.*

Photo / Pat Labadie, Lake Superior Marine Museum Archives, Superior Maritime Collections, UW-Superior

PROLOGUE

O N A VOYAGE ALONG THE SHIPWRECK COAST, I sailed over the bones of the *Edmund Fitzgerald*. She lay below me in her cold tomb under more than 500 feet of water. I pulled my foul weather parka closer about me on the bouncing deck of the sailboat I was in – but it was not the sea-like wind that chilled me.

It seemed inconceivable that any storm could have brought down this formidable steel ship, for her sheer size, modern design and construction made her seem indestructible to anything nature could throw at her. She had been designed to withstand hurricane-force blasts and shoulder aside the highest waves. She had proved herself with 748 voyages up and down the Great Lakes – more than a million miles – in all kinds of heavy weather.

But on November 10, 1975, the *Edmund Fitzgerald* sank so quickly she did not have time to cry out for help. All her crew went down with her in one of the most haunting of modern maritime mysteries. She is the *Titanic* of the Great Lakes, whose sudden death still sends chills down any sailor's backbone.

For years, I have been spellbound by the boat's death. I talked with the last men out on the lake in contact with the *Fitzgerald* and I had written about her last voyage. But a chance observation by an old lake captain had set me on a new course of investigation: what had happened inside the *aft-section* of the doomed ship?

It had been a remarkable battle by brave men, but there were no witnesses or survivors, so parts of their story have to be reconstructed. Using a little detective work, let us go now into the world of these gallant men in their final hours.

ROUTE OF THE FITZGERALD - - - - - - - - - - →

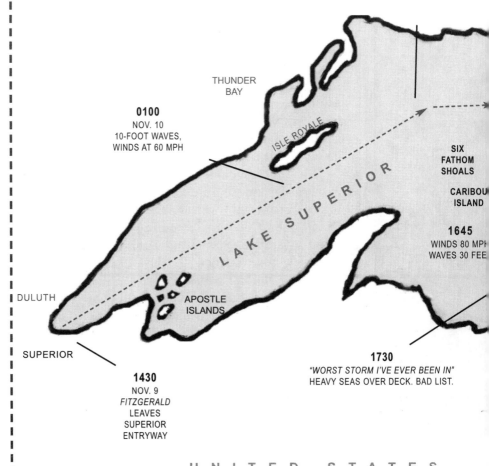

0700
NOV. 10.
WINDS SWITCH TO NORTHEAST

THUNDER
BAY

0100
NOV. 10
10-FOOT WAVES,
WINDS AT 60 MPH

ISLE ROYALE

SIX
FATHOM
SHOALS

CARIBOU
ISLAND

L A K E   S U P E R I O R

1645
WINDS 80 MPH
WAVES 30 FEET

DULUTH

APOSTLE
ISLANDS

SUPERIOR

1430
NOV. 9
FITZGERALD
LEAVES
SUPERIOR
ENTRYWAY

1730
"WORST STORM I'VE EVER BEEN IN"
HEAVY SEAS OVER DECK. BAD LIST.

U N I T E D   S T A T E S

C A N A D A

NOV. 10
1340
HEADING TOWARD
SIX FATHOM SHOALS

MICHIPICOTEN
ISLAND

1520
FITZGERALD IN
SHOAL AREA

1530
FITZGERALD TAKES
ON LIST

1915
FITZGERALD
SUDDENLY SINKS
WITH
ALL ABOARD

ILLUSTRATION BY MARLIN BREE

LAST RACE

OF THE

EDMUND
FITZGERALD

The crew of the "Big Fitz"
battle it out to the last

NOV. 10, 1520 HOURS: The *Edmund Fitzgerald* shuddered and seemed to stumble. She no longer had that sensation of flight through the breakers that were cresting above 18 feet.

In the wheelhouse, Captain Ernest M. McSorley stiffened. Beneath his feet, the steel deck had an odd vibration to it, and he felt a jolt in his knees. His body pitched forward and he grabbed a safety rail.

"Something's wrong, Captain." It was the wheelman.

"Steady." It was important to keep the pilothouse crew calm.

Captain McSorley's thick hair was plastered to his head. He lifted his hat, and ran his hand through it, then tugged it down securely on his sweat-stained brow. *Keep going,* he vowed to himself.

It had been a hard passage through a

quick rising northeaster that had gone round to the northwest. He and his crew had been fighting the late November storm last night and all day long. It was the worst storm of his memory, with howling winds and huge waves.

His fist thumped the sill of the spray-drenched pilothouse window. Out there, the sky was darkening as night came on. The lake seemed alive with raw menace

The sudden scraping noise, the vibration, the halting sensation meant only one thing: she had hit bottom. Somehow, somewhere, a reef had reached up to spear her plates.

The unthinkable horror had happened.

IT WAS A BAD TIME to be out on Lake Superior when the Witches of November came calling. This late in the shipping season, the terrible storms that rage across the world's largest freshwater lake had a history of sweeping boats and sailors down into the depths with their high winds and high waves.

But Nov. 9, 1975, had been unseasonably warm and muggy, an unusually pleasant Indian summer day. The big *Fitzgerald* slipped out the Superior entryway at 1:51 p.m., onto an unnaturally quiet lake.

Captain McSorley, impatient as ever to get underway on the long voyage to Detroit, had checked the weather forecasts. They called for south to southwest winds of 8 to 16 knots in the afternoon, becoming southeast to east, and increasing to 23 knots – gusty, but still good sailing.

He had that gut feeling something was brewing, but the Captain was not especially concerned. Heavy weather sailing had been part of his life as a sailor.

He had started on the lakes at age 18 as a deck boy and worked his way up through the ranks to become the youngest Captain on the lakes at age 37. He was now 62, and, his hair was still jet black. He was a tough old seaman, of medium height, barrel chested with big hands. He was a competitive, hard driver: the company expected a lake Captain to meet his schedules.

The *Fitz* was his special love. When she was launched in 1958, she was the advanced product of Great Lakes boat building with steel plates measuring up to an inch in thickness, a tough boat designed to take Superior's worst waves.

At 729 feet in length, she was the largest ship to be launched in the 50s and was among the fastest ore boats.

But after nearly two decades of storm and waves, she was showing some aging. She'd punched her way through millions of waves and fought her way through countless storms. She'd been loaded and unloaded thousands of times, and the loading docks were brutal: tons of taconite roared down the chutes into the hold and everyone on board could hear the *Fitz's* hull groan. She'd also had had her share of scrapes with piers and docks and a large crease in the plates on her starboard side bore witness to her latest encounter. The lakers led a hard life.

But the old girl was still sound and strong, and still relatively young for an ore boat. She regularly passed her Coast Guard certifications.

As Captain McSorley steamed onto the lake through the Superior entryway, his men were still working on deck. The heavy steel hatch covers, each 11 feet by 48 feet and weighing 12,000 pounds, had already been lifted into place by a special crane on deck. They fit over massive coamings, as thick as the hull plating. There were 21 hatches; each hatch had 68 manually closed clamps. Typically, not all clamps were fastened if a boat got underway in a hurry, for the men could fasten the clamps after they cleared port.

Captain McSorley did not worry about the hatches. The *Fitz* was built to take waves on her "weather deck." If water came aboard during storms, it would simply press down harder on the coamings. The more water, the harder they pressed.

The *Fitzgerald's* hatches were rugged and proven. In all her years on the lakes, the big boat had never arrived in harbor with a wet cargo hold.

N ov. 10, 1445 HOURS: As the *Fitz* steamed past Michipicoten Island on a new course shaped up to pass to the east of the rocks off Caribou Island, Captain McSorley peered out into the maelstrom. Clouds of snow swirled over the stormy seas waves and he could see only a few hundred feet ahead.

It had been a bad passage so far. The eerie calm and clammy warmth of the day before had exploded into a late-season storm. By 1 a.m., black water had begun to scour the *Fitz's* deck. The barometer kept dropping, and, the storm cell intensified with 60 mph. winds. The seas were building rapidly from the northwest. He could hear and feel the waves as they worked their way across his boat.

From his castle-like pilothouse, he looked aft to see that waves were crawling up on the *Fitzgerald's* weather deck and rolling down the length. She was regularly squirming as the waves hit her starboard aft section, moved her over a bit, then made her heel under their impact.

They'd compress the hatch covers tighter under their tons of weight; then they'd rush to the forward superstructure. With a boom, they'd hit the Texas deck and rear up to the pilothouse with their foam splashing the windows. Their weight would push the bow section down a little, and, Captain McSorley could feel the *Fitz* move under him. He'd brace himself and wait patiently to be rewarded moments later as the bow sprang up once again, ready to do battle with the next set of waves.

He studied the wave crests as they came toward him, timing them. They were roaring like freight trains, the crests hitting every six seconds. That meant they were moving at about 25 to 30 miles per hour. Incredible energy, thousands of tons of pressure, was slamming into his long boat in several areas at once. The troughs between waves were growing and that meant special problems. If the boat were to be suspended between waves, and have her mid-section sink into a trough, she could crack her back. That happened on the long ships.

The wheelsman struggled to keep the *Fitz* on course. The boat was alive with horrific forces at work and even the massive *Fitz* could broach in seas like this. If she turned sideways to the oncoming seas, they could totally overpower and overwhelm her.

There. He saw it again.

The front end of the boat had flexed, and then wandered off to port. All ore boats twist in waves, just as a tall flagpole bends in the wind, but the *Fitzgerald* had a bad case of the meanders.

She had a loose keel. Her bottom hull plate had broken away from the massive keel structure that was supposed to keep her strong. The year before, a crewmember down in her bilge had shoved a crowbar between the keel and the hull – where they should have been welded together. Instead of a solid, continuous weld, the keel was welded to the hull with small tack, or strip, welds. Some of the welds had cracked or broken.

The shipyard had welded some strips of metal to fill in the gaps between the keel and the hull. She was OK'd for use, but the crew secretly worried that the fix didn't fully repair the hull.

Also, the legal limit for her cargo-carrying capacity had been increased. That meant she had more weight to carry on her keel – putting more stress on her hull.

The captain and the crew noticed that when the *Fitz* lay deeper in the water, her "wiggling thing" got worse.

In the growing storm waves, it seemed to Captain McSorley that the bow section moved around more than ever before. He'd been in the aft section on previous voyages, checking the bow's movement. From the aft section, he could look forward over the huge expanse of weather deck, then see the forward section move off to one side as the boat fought her way through heavy weather.

She'd move off, hesitate, and slowly come back.

Now, in the worst weather the veteran Captain had ever seen, she was definitely in harm's way. The wiggling thing meant that her "loose keel" was coming further adrift and his boat could be in serious trouble.

He had already checked down a little to about 14 mph. to ease his laboring hull.

T HE WAVES WERE GIVING THE LONG HULL A TWIST. Maybe if he could get behind Caribou Island, he'd put the island between him and the waves. Then he'd be in the lee of the island, heading for the mainland, and give his hard-laboring boat some ease.

But with his radar out, and, snow flurries starting, he could not make out any landmark to guide by. The windows were starting to ice up and the lake felt like a stranger.

His navigation was by dead reckoning that somehow had to account for the prodding of the wave trains that kept throwing the ship off course. Keeping an accurate course went out the window with the waves and the wind. The wind shoved the boat along; the waves gave it a little boost before they ran down the spar deck.

True speed over the bottom was difficult to estimate under these conditions, much less determine the exact course made good. The best the helmsman and the captain could do was count on their knowledge and intuition.

They knew somewhere to the starboard lay the reefs off Caribou Island. They'd passed Six Fathom Shoals many times before.

They only needed to give them the usual berth – say, a mile or so.

A NOTHER GROAN shuddered through the *Fitz*. The bow rolled like a freight train going around a curve, then came back up slowly, her hull crying out her pain.

In the pilothouse, as the windows moaned and rattled, Captain McSorley knew it was time to get to shelter. The radio had been alive with messages from captains out in the storm. Already one ore boat had gotten off the lake and taken refuge in Thunder Bay; another had sought shelter off Isle Royal. Behind the *Fitz*, about 10 miles away, the *Anderson* doggedly plunged ahead.

From his position to the north and west of Caribou Island, Captain McSorley knew that the locks at Sault Ste. Marie would be impassable – huge waves would be rolling at the entryway. That left Whitefish Point as a place of refuge. He'd give the reefs at the Point a wide berth, and, then head in toward land and drop anchor. The Point would bear the brunt of the storm and the waves. In sheltered waters, his big boat would ride easy until the storm passed.

He peered into the horizon. During November, there was little enough light, and with the snows billowing past the waves, visibility was limited. Darkness was coming on fast

D OWN IN THE ENGINE ROOM, below the water's surface, the battle with the storm was personal. In a steel hull, sound transmits greatly. Even above the whine of the turbines and the thump of the propeller, the crew in the aft section could hear the big combers colliding with the *Fitz's* stern. They banged, thumped, and, roared.

It was like being inside a giant steel kettledrum.

No one looked up from work, but their senses were tautly attuned for any major change or threat. They were acutely aware of the big waves banging against their ship, for no one felt the labors of the big ore boat more than the aft-section gang. Unlike the captain in his steel tower forward atop the ship's bow, the crew worked inside the hull, submerged below the waterline. They heard and felt everything.

The engine room rose like an open cathedral from the keel to the top of the deckhouse. In its bottom lay its two great turbines, boilers and propeller shaft. The huge atrium was the home of the engineers of the *Fitz*, monitoring engine rpm's, steam pressure, and, boiler temperature.

In the heavy seas, the aft section labored and groaned. Every rise and fall resonated agonizingly with the deep-thumping noise of the propeller.

Listening carefully, the chief engineer kept a tight fist on the throttle. As a wave hit, the stern would rise, sometimes lifting the huge propeller partly out of the water. The propeller would begin to speed up out of control until the chief throttled down the shaft revolutions.

It was constant, careful seamanship, feeling the rise of the stern, listening to the thrashing of the giant propeller, watching the shaft revolutions on the gauge and adjusting the speed. Sometimes if he misgauged, the prop came too far out of the water and shook the whole ship. The strain on the *Fitz's* battle scared hull bothered him.

S IX FATHOM SHOALS, a series of underwater reefs extending five miles northeast of Caribou Island, is an area well known to lake captains. On the northern trek, ore boats routinely cross within several miles of the shoals. On some pilothouse charts, the mate simply draws a heavy red dot on this area. *Danger!* Stay out!

Based on 1916 soundings, which largely were derived by dragging a chain and other primitive measuring devices over the bottom, Canadian Lake Superior Chart 2310 showed a series of underwater reefs extending out about five miles north from Caribou island, some as little as six fathoms deep.

What the chart did not show was a reef that lay about one mile further to the east, within five and a quarter fathoms from the surface. That 32 feet of depth was enough for most ore boats to slide easily over without touching.

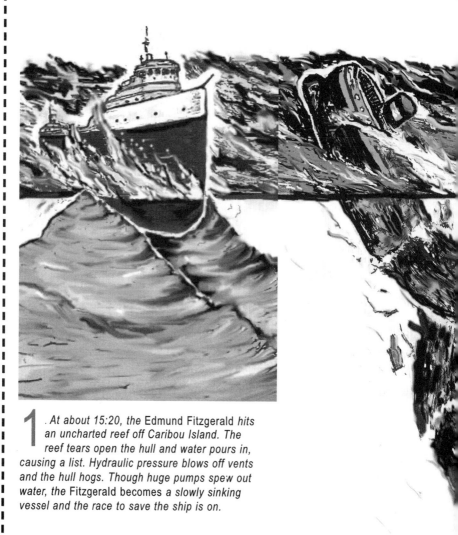

1. *At about 15:20, the Edmund Fitzgerald hits an uncharted reef off Caribou Island. The reef tears open the hull and water pours in,* causing a list. Hydraulic pressure blows off vents and the hull hogs. Though huge pumps spew out water, *the Fitzgerald becomes a slowly sinking vessel and the race to save the ship is on.*

2. *At about 19:15, the Fitzgerald suddenly plunges bow-first to the bottom 530 feet down, carrying all crew members with her.* Her end comes so quickly, she does not have time to cry out for help. She remains intact going down, but when her bow strikes, the 729-foot vessel's cargo shifts and the hull breaks apart under the impact.

3. *The 253-foot aft section turns over, lying bottom up. The 276-foot forward section sits upright, as if ready to sail on. In between lies a junkyard, all that is left of the torn mid-section. All of the Fitzgerald's crew perished with her in her fatal plunge.*

ILLUSTRATIONS/ MARLIN BREE

But that was in clear weather and calm seas. Now the reef lay like granite teeth below the storm waves that curled the surface.

NOV. 10: 1520 HOURS. The *Fitz* seemed to be groaning aloud as her bow dug in one way and her powerful aft section pushed her forward another way. It was a series of creak, moan, grind, popping sounds as hull steel compressed against the pressure and fingers of tension began working against the welds that held the hull to the heavy keel members. It was like a god of the sea was taking the giant boat in his hands and was slowly twisting it one way, then another.

In the pilothouse, Captain McSorley glanced at the ship's clock as it neared 3:20 pm. The ominous gray day would turn black soon.

Suddenly, there was a new sound. It came above all the other noises of the boat and the storm, and, it was unmistakable – the grating of steel plates against rock. Captain McSorley felt the pitch and sway of the pilothouse below his feet cease and the forward momentum of their flight stop. He felt the pressure against his feet, pressed to the steel deck, and his knees buckled forward.

Mother of God.

The vibrations of the indescribable rumbled up to him. His old fears came to him: somehow, they had touched bottom. How could that be? He was a mile off from all known reefs. Six Fathom Shoals should lay to the west of him.

He did some quick calculations in his head: Six fathoms equaled 36 feet. The *Fitz* drew 27 feet forward, 29 ½ feet aft, so even if she were off course and crossed too near the reefs, she could still slide by with nine to 6 ½ feet to spare.

But that was her depth in dead calm weather. They were in mostly thirty-foot waves by now, with the boat bouncing up and down in their fury. Perhaps she had bounced down too far and touched bottom.

But that wouldn't account for this!

Another ominous thought came to him: maybe the old charts didn't account for all the reefs.

Maybe he had just found a new reef. *Sweet Jesus!*

STEEL BOATS ARE NOISY, especially the big ones. In the harbor, the belowdecks crew can listen to the tickle of the water against their hulls. Underway, they can hear the gurgle of water moving past their waterlines and if there are waves, they can hear them thump the metal plates. In heavy weather, the sound intensifies. The aft-section gang can hear a sound like steel drums being pounded by giant sledgehammers – a sound that reverberates unmuffled through the long hull. They can hear the roaring of the waves, the crash of the heavy water against the hull, and the sound of a waterfall rolling along the spar deck.

What they heard now was a raw, primordial sound. The growl of steel on granite became a loud screech and a piercing groan as heavy steel plates bent and tore.

The ship shuddered and partially slowed. Instantly, the belowdecks crew knew:

They had hit and hit hard.

BRACING HIMSELF, Captain McSorley spun around and dashed to the aft section of the pilothouse. His practiced eye looked down over the spar deck and he was only somewhat relieved: he still had a boat under him.

Perhaps the bottom had glanced across something down there, and the plates were dented. That'd happened before to him and to other ore boats, grounding out in the St. Mary's river. Scuttlebut had it that some ore boats had lightly touched bottom here when they got in too close to the shoals.

But as a wave cleared from the deck, he saw fence cable twisted and lying broken on deck, somewhere forward of the midsection. The steel stanchions that held the cable had twisted inward, evidence of great force that no wave could muster.

The fence wire was half-inch diameter steel cable held tautly, but not tight, through the stanchions. The fence was to provide safety on the sides of the deck so crew wouldn't slip overboard. Now it lay twisting in the waves. He could see the strands of wire, waving about.

Not far aft from the pilothouse, several topside vents were missing. Between waves, they were rolling about the decks. Captain McSorley knew that boarding waves alone could never have broken those heavy metal castings.

As realization hit, he began to perspire. It had not just been a light grounding, but a colossal impact down below. He had felt part of it in the forward section. Enormous pressure had blasted up from the ballast tanks at the very bottom of the vessel and compressed air inside the tanks from the impact had torn off the cast metal vents. The air had come up so fast it couldn't get out the tops and they blew off.

His eyes went back to the fence rail writhing in the broken water. That could only be accounted for if the *Fitz*'s middle section had been hogged from the impact with some terrible force. Even the heavy cables couldn't stretch enough.

"Captain, we're taking on a list." It was the wheelman.

They were leaning to starboard, little bit by little bit. From atop the tower of the pilothouse, the Captain could feel the incline increasing. He knew that the spar deck was lowering its starboard side to the waves. That would let big waves come aboard more easily, and, put more water on the deck. . .

"Turn on the pumps," he ordered, bracing himself against the tilt of the deck. Below, two huge pumps began to howl, each capable of throwing out 28 tons of water every minute.

THE *FITZGERALD'S* ENGINEERS reported that the hull was taking on water from somewhere directly aft of the pilothouse. It was the starboard side, since the hull was listing in that direction, but they couldn't get to the leak since it lay beneath the load of taconite they carried.

Captain McSorley shook his head wearily. His boat was in trouble.

He had hoped that she had suffered damage only to the hull plates under her Number 1 ballast tank, on the starboard side. Since she was running with a full load of taconite, that ballast tank was empty; if she had water filling it, then it would give her a list. But that water could be contained.

But if she had struck hard enough, she could have damaged both her bottom as well as her ballast tank. He pondered the imponderable: how many tons of water could cause a 729-foot ship carrying 26,116 tons of taconite to list?

Captain McSorley picked up the mike and radioed the *Anderson* fighting her way 10 miles behind him:

"*Arthur M. Anderson*, this is the *Fitzgerald*. I have sustained some topside damage; I have some fence rail down, two vents lost or damaged, and I have taken on a list. I am checking down. Will you stand by?"

The captain of the *Anderson,* Bernie Cooper, paused only a moment to calculate what that meant. "Roger on that," he said. "Do you have your pumps going?"

"Yes, " McSorley snapped. "Both of them."

Both skippers now knew that the *Fitzgerald* was in deep trouble.

CAPTAIN MCSORLEY was grim. Huge seas had boarded the *Fitzgerald* and she was taking on water. From the reports he was getting from the aft section, he knew that conditions for the belowdecks crew were hellish. He knew they would get worse.

He was on the radio when he spotted something out of the corner of his eye. Some of the crew had left the aft deckhouse.

"Don't allow nobody on deck," he yelled to his first mate.

Conditions in the aft section had become so bad that some crewmembers were trying to get the lifeboats ready.

Though the *Anderson* was following in their track, Captain McSorley knew that there was no hope of ship-to-ship rescue. The two vessels could not come together in these seas without the big boats banging into one another. One, or perhaps both, vessels could suffer great damage.

Even if the *Fitz* could launch its lifeboats, the small, open boats would be overpowered and capsize in the huge waves. If they survived the breakers, chances were the crew would die of cold and the exposure.

They would have to ride it out – there was no other option.

AS NIGHT FELL, the *Fitz*'s spotlights illuminated a hellish scene. Waves that seemed as big as mountains overran the aft section and shoved their way onto the spar deck. They put their enormous weight on the big *Fitz's* hatches and mid section and then piled up high behind the pilothouse. The waves made the whole ship twist and tremble.

Captain McSorley grabbed a handhold to steady himself. The deck tilted hard to starboard; it was difficult to keep a footing on the slippery floor, much less stand upright. The only way to keep from being thrown about was to brace your feet wide apart, and, hang on.

Each movement caused the wheelsman to struggle with the rudder; the *Fitz* was heavy, out of trim, and not responding well in the heavy seas. She slewed to starboard and there was no way to keep her exactly on course.

Captain McSorley worked his way to the chartroom at the back of the pilothouse and double-checked his nautical chart: Less than 18 miles to go to Whitefish Point. At their rate of speed, they'd get behind Whitefish Point in less than an hour and a half.

He peered to the southeast, looking anxiously for the Whitefish Point lighthouse, whose beacon could guide his ship to safety. The beacon was dark.

Unknown to him, the storm had ripped out the lighthouse's electricity.

THE LONG NIGHT DEEPENED. Outside the pilothouse windows, the waves seemed to rear higher and more menacing than ever. The spotlights illumined the monsters as they struck, covering the glass with spray and black water.

Some were looming higher than the pilothouse and Captain McSorley could only look in awe. It was the peak of the storm.

Captain McSorley made radio contact again: "It's the worst sea I've ever been in."

THE BOW OF THE *FITZ* was going down, as if she were on a slow escalator, then slowly recovering. The list to starboard had grown worse, and, it seemed to Captain McSorley as if he were trying to stand on a hill's slope.

Below him, unseen, black water was growing inside the ship. The pumps could not get rid of it fast enough.

His big ship was in the fight of its life. Giant waves were routinely overrunning her lowered starboard spar deck and standing as high as 12 feet on the weather deck. At times, she felt like she was a submarine.

He was on a southeast heading now, with the winds rolling out of the north-northwest. The hellish winds were topping 98 mph.

Only 17 miles to go.

He could sense the land, somewhere out there in the raging darkness. Get around the Point, and off this black wilderness of water, and he could find shelter for his laboring, wounded boat. He could anchor behind the Point and handle her flooding problems. Or he could even run her bow aground.

He had options now. The race was nearly over.

F ROM WHERE THEY HUNG ON BELOW, the aft section crew felt every motion, heard every booming wave. It was difficult to stand without holding onto something, to keep from falling. They listened to the roaring of the waves, the crash of the heavy water against the hull, and the sound of a waterfall rolling along the spar deck.

One thing seemed clear: the waves were getting bigger, and, they were getting closer together.

Already, some water was running the length of the bilges. They could hear tons of water cascading back and forth inside the hull, back toward the aft section bulkheads. They could hear it gurgling below and, looking down, they could see the black, frothing liquid splashing in the bilge. In the shambling, rolling gait of the big boat, some of the chill water would slice up against the hot turbines and boilers, raising steam that billowed white.

The bilge pumps were howling; they could hear their powerful whine above the sound of the waves. As the stern lifted to a breaker, the pumps would speed up and make a sucking noise as water shifted forward through the boat.

The hellish night below decks continued.

O N THE *ANDERSON,* Captain Cooper felt his ship lurch, and, he instinctively twisted about to look back over the spar deck. To his horror, he saw a monster wall of water – bigger than anything yet – cover his entire vessel aft and then rush toward him. Black water piled up behind his pilothouse. Immediately, he felt his big ship's bow go down under the weight, groaning as she plowed her stem deeper into the cold water.

A horrible moment passed before the *Anderson's* bow fought its way skyward, shaking water off her back like a big dog. A second giant wave followed the first.

When the waves cleared off the boat, Captain Cooper saw that the torrent of water had damaged his aft lifeboat and torn off parts of her steel cabin superstructure. That meant one of the waves had to be at least 35 feet high – a monster wall of water.

Slowly, he turned his eyes forward as the huge waves raced down the lake. He felt a warning prickling on the back of his neck. Ahead, and in the direct path of the monster waves, was the struggling and wounded *Fitzgerald.*

HOW ARE WE DOING, CAPTAIN?" It was the chief engineer, valiantly working the throttle back in the engine room. Over the intercom, Captain McSorley could hear the *Fitz's* 7,500 horse-power steam turbine howling. The four-bladed, twenty-foot diameter bronze propeller was shuddering and cavitating as it lifted in and out of the water.

"We're gaining," Captain McSorley said, largely to keep up morale. Reflexively, he nodded toward where he hoped the distant headland would offer the boat shelter, just beyond the lighthouse at Whitefish Point.

He couldn't see anything in the darkness, but the snowstorm seemed to swirl in clouds beyond the pilothouse's windows. He figured he'd make out the lighthouse's beacon soon enough, not realizing that the light was out in the storm.

"You giving me all she's got?" he added. He glanced at the engine order telegraph, now set on the all-ahead full position.

"Full ahead," the engineer said. "Aye, sir."

Captain McSorley exhaled deeply. The long ordeal was about to end.

1910 HOURS: Out of nowhere in the furious snow squall, the giant wave train appeared, rumbling across the aft section. It easily straddled *Fitzgerald's* downward canting spar deck, covered it and roared forward. Its weight was incalculable: a thundering wall of water that piled up its tons of power directly behind the pilothouse.

On the bridge, Captain McSorley turned as he felt its weight, heard its rumble, and saw the looming green water coming at him. It was a big wave – bigger than all the others. Beneath his feet, he felt the bow sink as the *Fitz* struggled to stay afloat. He waited for it to shrug off the wave, then, rise again.

A second wave, bigger than the first, boarded the *Fitz*. It hissed like a serpent, a living thing, with a crown of foam, and headed for the pilothouse, even before the first wave had completely run off.

The big ship groaned anew with the weight. Captain McSorley felt it too; it felt like the weight of mountains upon his straining boat. Anxiously, he waited for the bow to regain buoyancy and come back up.

Beneath his feet, the deck began to slant forward as the second wave's crest – over 35 feet high – ran toward the pilothouse. Beneath its tons of water, the hatches moaned, but clamped tighter under tons of pressure to their steel coamings.

The seas filled the air with their coldness and their foam. Captain McSorley grabbed harder on his handhold as he felt his feet slip on the deck beneath him.

He turned around to face forward. In the yellow shine of the searchlights, the monsters grew larger and larger, surging upward to the bridge's square windows. He hung on as the bow disappeared like a submarine. He was about to say something to the wheelsman when the water suddenly filled the bridge's glass with a green, incandescent light. Captain McSorley could only stare at its horrible beauty.

He heard the awful gurgle and rush of water and then the pressure burst the glass, shattering it. A thundering wall of water roared inward, catching Captain McSorley in the chest, flinging him backwards in its terrible surge. The wheelman glanced up from the compass at the sound of the breaking glass, and clutched the wheel for a moment, bracing himself. His hands were torn away as the pressure swept him backward.

The burst of water swept everyone into the back of the cabin, slamming them into the unyielding steel of the pilothouse.

THE BOAT SHUDDERED AND BUCKED as it plunged into the howling seas. The bow caught at an angle, multiplying the force, jamming the hull with a wrenching twist. The force of the water was unrelenting: the first two hatches began to buckle inward in a V and implode in an explosion of water.

Inside the hull, a wall of water thundered forward. It roared past the screen bulkheads, hardly slowing down in their metal mesh. The bow tripped   under the weight, and, as it inclined more, the *Fitz's* cargo of taconite pellets, rounded like oversized metal shot pellets, rolled forward. The *Fitzgerald* gained speed as she made her great lunge downward.

THE MEN IN THE AFT SECTION heard the rumble, then felt the crash of the giant wave on the aft section deckhouse. It had never been designed for this kind of boarding wave, and the steel plates dented inward.

As the rogue wave climbed higher, it slammed against the after deckhouse's doors, which had been dogged shut. There was a rush of water around the steel frames as Superior spurted inside and ran down the steel steps in a torrent. Belowdecks, the men looked up at the cascade, hoping not only the door, but also the entire aft deckhouse would survive the impossible seas.

Portlights shattered, letting a fire hose of water into the deckhouse and down into the crew's dining area. The men looked for anything to hang onto, but their feet kept getting swept from beneath them. The cook looked at the crash of glass and broken pottery to see a gush of water push itself into the galley, slam onto the hot stove, and turn into steam. It scattered the quick meal he was preparing and dumped it onto the floor. He grabbed for the galley table, and, held his balance. He watched as even the deeply fiddled coffee pot on the stove turned over.

The aft section seemed to slew to port. The "wiggling thing" that previously had bedeviled the bow section now was back to threaten them. The loose plates in the keel, trembling under the pressure of the aft section avalanche of water, was now letting the stern wander off.

The whole motion of the hull had altered. First there was the noise, the shove to port, and then the horrible groaning.

There was a strange rush of water outside the hull – ominous and long and then the stern began to elevate high into the air. The crewmen felt the change, rather than saw it. There was the sound of metal grating as the boat increased its angle. In the galley, dishes, coffee pots, and loose pans all headed forward. The cook grabbed a rail as the ship began to stand on its head.

The giant prop began to speed up, but was checked by the engineer. As it went underwater again, he added more power and the big prop dug in, giving the ship forward momentum.

Despite the steam and the sloshing water, the boilers were fired up, the turbines hummed and the prop shaft revolved.

But now the waves were silent.

The men waited. The bow would rise, the *Fitz* would get back on course, and she'd battle onward.

Suddenly, their world turned black and upside down.

CAREENING INTO THE DEPTHS, the *Fitzgerald's* bow plunged over 500 feet at a speed of about 30 mph. It smashed at an angle into the bottom mud, dug in to a depth of 25 feet until it hit bedrock and jolted forward.

Inch-thick steel twisted and ruptured in the *Fitzgerald's* damaged bottom. Its re-welded, rusted spine bent grotesquely.

Twenty six thousand tons of taconite pellets exploded forward. The screen bulkheads burst, letting the pellets out like a huge cannon blast and the *Fitzgerald* burst apart. The red, green and white navigation lights went out forever.

The center section spread wreckage over a two-acre area. Hatches came askew, some blasted by the force of compressed air during her sinking; others hammered off by tons of taconite. The area resembled a junkyard more than a sunken ship.

Immediately in front of the pile, the front section of the *Fitzgerald* came to rest upright, as if ready to sail off. Her battered bow showed the terrible impact, crumpled heavily on the starboard side.

Behind the junkyard, the 253-foot long aft section was still under steam when she crashed into the bottom. The torque of her propeller swiveled her about, and she landed upside down in the bottom.

Inside the aft section, some of her crew were still conscious in their underwater tomb, searching for a pocket of air. Upside down, in the cold and dark, they faced the horror of every sailor: to be trapped deep underwater, with no hope of escape.

The propeller stopped turning, the water gushed in, and, soon all was still.

In the pilothouse, the engine order telegraph was still set in the all-ahead full position.

But the *Fitzgerald* had lost its great race.

EPILOGUE

A FEW YEARS AGO, I was talking to a retired ore boat captain and an old friend of mine about the last hours of the *Fitzgerald*. I was curious about one part of testimony that had come out during the Coast Guard hearings. In a radio transmission overheard by Capt. Woodard, the Captain of the *Fitzgerald* had ordered that none of the crew be allowed on deck about an hour after the doomed vessel had crossed the reefs.

"Why'd he say that?" I asked.

The old captain's face grew thoughtful as he replied in a very quiet voice:

"They were trying to get off."

It was his opinion, of course, but the best one I'd heard to explain why some of the aft-section crew was on deck during the storm. Conditions were so bad that they were willing to brave the huge waves and struggle in the freezing water to get to their lifeboat.

That had given me a remarkable insight into the crew of the *Fitzgerald*. Though a lot has been written about the captain and the men of the pilot house, very little has been written about the crew and their monumental, but loosing battle in the aft section of the doomed ship. Their last hours were worthy of special focus.

W HAT HAD GONE WRONG? I was no newcomer to the tale of the *Fitzgerald*. I had already come across quite a bit of information as I sailed the shores of Lake Superior. When I had tied up in remote locations, alongside docks, barges and tugboats, I had gotten to know some of the big lake's views. Watermen and sailors told me tales of the fateful day that the *Fitz* went down. None of them believed the Coast Guard's board's report that she sank primarily because of hatch cover failures.

To be fair, that was only one of several possible explanations to the sinking of the *Fitzgerald*. The Board's official report served to set off a bout of other explanations and arguments. I've heard most of them.

Here's a rundown on various theories and opinions, along with my own evaluations:

Hatches gave way. According to this theory, the boarding waves during the storm were of such a size that the *Fitzgerald's* hatch covers could not sustain the weight and collapsed, letting massive amounts of water in the hull. This occurred, according to the argument, at about the time the *Fitzgerald* first reported problems of a list.

In my opinion, there is little to sustain this argument since the other ships, which had similar hatches, came through the storm without hatch cover failure. Nor did Captain McSorley state that he had suffered hatch cover damage when he radio'd other ships. Note that he was specific in reporting a list, fence rail down, and, even broken vents. Something as large as a hatch would easily be noticeable to him, and, he would have reported it along with other problems.

In a report filed after the Coast Guard report, the Lake Owners Association carefully framed a rebuttal to the hatch cover analysis, reporting that there had been no known problems with the newer steel hatch covers such as were on the *Fitzgerald*. In other words, the hatch covers had survived the wave.

My feeling is that the two forward hatch covers that had caved in and folded into a v-shape in the sunken forward section were damaged not on the surface but when she made her fatal dive. At that time, the speed of her dive and the pressure of the water had burst them in.

Hull failure: That the *Fitzgerald* had hull flaws including the re-welded "loose keel" is fairly well accepted. Rather than still being the Queen of the Fleet, as common legend has it, the ship was an aging vessel that had been driven hard. Captain McSorley was known to be a hard master and, not one to slow down for weather.

In her final year, she had incurred a large gash along her starboard side after a collision with an abutment. Someone had sent me a photograph of that damage. People on the lake who saw her during her last years reported her to be a "rust bucket." I'd also heard reports from friends and relatives of the *Fitzgerald* crewmen, who said their loved ones had a good deal of apprehension about late season sailing with her "wriggling thing."

Captain McSorley himself had been concerned about the big ship's ultra flexing in big waves.

"The wiggling thing," Captain McSorley once was reported as saying, "scares me."

A crewmember described it as like "a diving board after somebody has jumped off."

But sometimes, the bow didn't straighten back until minutes later. There was a definite structural problem here, but had the "loose keel" finally detached itself from the plates, the *Fitz* likely would have broken up and sunk in a different manner than the one in which she did.

As it was, she began having problems only after she crossed the reefs.

Rogue wave: There is no question that huge waves engulfed the *Anderson* and later the *Fitzgerald.* When I talked with Captain Cooper, he told me that they were like a tidal wave – big enough to reach over the aft section and damage parts of her superstructure and a lifeboat before overrunning the deck. He told me he had green water standing as high as 12 feet on the spar deck, making it seem more like a submarine than an ore carrier.

Minutes later, the same waves overran the *Fitz.* However, the waves alone should not have sunk the big ore carrier, since they sank no other ships out on the lake that day. In my opinion, a the big waves that came aboard the *Fitz* were the final step in a series of disasters that had befallen the doomed boat — the proverbial straw that broke the camel's back.

The *Fitz* at that time had massive problems battling an incoming gusher of water and was sinking lower and lower in the water, nearing perhaps neutral buoyancy, with her bow depressed. The big waves rolling easily over her stern and up her canting spar deck to be dammed up behind the tall pilothouse were probably the final disaster to befall her.

Big trough: The theory here is that in big storms, a trough forms between wave crests so that the hull of a large ship becomes "suspended" between the peaks. This leaves the center of the long hull unsupported, and, cracks the keelson and the hull. From reports I received, this has happened to other ore boats, but has not resulted in the sinking of one, though boats have come into port with "cracked keels."

Broken up on the surface: One argument has it that the *Fitzgerald* broke up on the surface of Superior in the storm. In the instance where a ship has broken up on the surface, such as the case of the *Daniel J. Morrell*, the two ends separated and later were found underwater many miles apart.

Though the bow section sank near the site of the breakup, the *Morrell's* stern section lies on the bottom of Lake Michigan in about 200 feet of water, after having traveled about *five miles* after the breakup.

On the other hand, the *Fitzgerald's* 276-foot front section rests within 170 feet of the 253-foot aft section, a relatively compact area. If she had broken up at the surface, her hull sections would have scattered over a wide area, as did the *Morrell*.

Evidence of the reef: If you want to find out what happened to the *Fitzgerald*, goes this theory, stop looking at the hull. Look instead at the reef she hit.

That reef lies about five miles northeast of Caribou Island at 47 26 47N and 85 48 41 W. It is a "new" reef that was added to charts by a Canadian survey the following spring after the *Fitzgerald* sank and is among a cluster of reefs with soundings of 8 and 9 fathoms. But the "new reef" is only 5 ¼ fathoms from the surface – shallow enough for an ore boat to bottom out in storm conditions.

Years back, I had attempted to launch a diving investigation on the reef. Plans for that expedition fell through, but the concept was good – for an impartial group of amateur divers to go down and actually look at the reef that the *Fitz* was supposed to have hit. The reef tip would be only about 30 feet down – an easy dive.

If a 729-foot steel ship carrying 26,117 tons of taconite had hit the reef, I figured, it must have left some evidence. There would be the impact of the steel upon the rock, leaving a gouge in the usual scum and film that covers most underwater rocks. In fact, bright rock might still show.

The hull would have left some other marks: the *Fitz's* bottom paint, for example, would have been scraped off on the reef. There might have been metal pieces lying about from where she was holed and where she had scraped her metal plates. Maybe she left rust flakes and taconite pellets may have erupted from her

ruptured hull. As one diver ominously told me: she probably left more than her calling card.

My diving party wasn't the only one interested in taking a look at the reef. The rumor I had heard was that a professional diver had been hired to go down and look for any evidence of impact the following spring, while things were fresh down there. After that, the story gets a little fuzzy – with conspiracy buffs claiming that the diver was hired by an insurance company and after making his confidential finding, told to keep his silence. He did that.

Summing up: The number one factor in the *Fitzgerald's* sinking was her contact with the previously unchartered "new" reef which lies 5 ¼ fathoms below the surface of the water in the area of Six Fathom Shoals off Caribou Island.

Before she went into that area, she had no problems; after she came out of that area, she reported severe problems including fence rail down, a list, and, broken vents – all indicators of major hull problems that could only mean she had hit something. The reefs, including the "new" reef in Six Fathom Shoals, were the only things in her way.

After striking the reef, probably in the vicinity of the hull's starboard bottom section aft of the pilothouse, she was a slowly sinking, but valiant ship. She might have made it to the protection of Whitefish Point had she not been overrun by the rogue waves. The waves easily came aboard her lowered spar deck, depressing the center section, and rolling along until they piled high behind the pilothouse – probably to the horror of the captain and the crew.

The hatches still held, but the bow section was depressed by the weight into the water, and it began its downward plunge to the bottom. In the parlance of the lake, she "submarined."

Water inside her hull ran forward. Still intact, the doomed vessel powered forward underwater, engines running until the bow hit hard on the bottom. Her already limber hull was wracked by shifting ore bursting forward and outward.

The bow section dug in, and, came to rest upright, as if she were still sailing forward. The center section became a vast junkyard of torn metal, loose hatch covers and piles of ore. Twisted by the still-turning propeller, the aft section turned over, and, came to lie upside down with her bottom pointed toward the surface.

THERE IS YET ANOTHER MYSTERY to the *Fitzgerald*. In one of the last expeditions to explore the wreck, a submersible went down for a stereo-video recording of the pilothouse. One curious thing that the video captured was that the pilothouse door *was locked* in the open position. A short distance from the hull, on the bottom of the lake, rested the body of a man, lying face down.

The unmistakable conclusion was that, somehow, a crewmember had survived the ride to the bottom. He had opened the pilothouse door, dogged it, and possibly with his last burst of strength, gotten out at 500 feet below the surface – to his ultimate doom. He now rests beside his ship.

For more information on the sinking of the Fitzgerald, check out the Author's Notes at the back of the book.

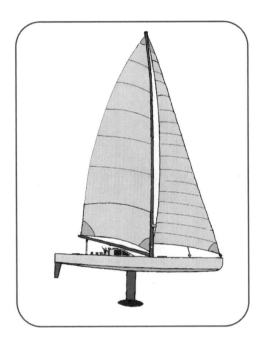

FIVE

THE
PASSION
OF
MIKE PLANT

At the helm of his speeding ocean racer: A smiling Mike Plant.

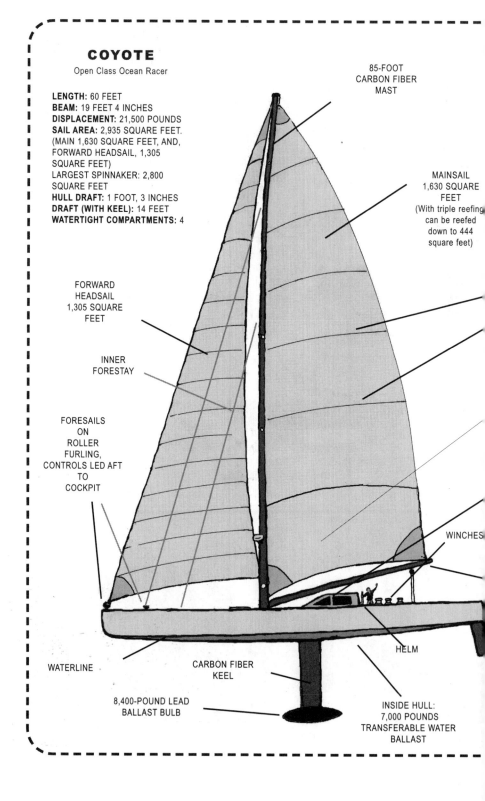

COYOTE

Open Class Ocean Racer

LENGTH: 60 FEET
BEAM: 19 FEET 4 INCHES
DISPLACEMENT: 21,500 POUNDS
SAIL AREA: 2,935 SQUARE FEET.
(MAIN 1,630 SQUARE FEET, AND,
FORWARD HEADSAIL, 1,305
SQUARE FEET)
LARGEST SPINNAKER: 2,800
SQUARE FEET
HULL DRAFT: 1 FOOT, 3 INCHES
DRAFT (WITH KEEL): 14 FEET
WATERTIGHT COMPARTMENTS: 4

85-FOOT
CARBON FIBER
MAST

MAINSAIL
1,630 SQUARE
FEET
(With triple reefing
can be reefed
down to 444
square feet)

FORWARD
HEADSAIL
1,305 SQUARE
FEET

INNER
FORESTAY

FORESAILS
ON
ROLLER
FURLING,
CONTROLS LED AFT
TO
COCKPIT

WINCHES

HELM

WATERLINE

CARBON FIBER
KEEL

8,400-POUND LEAD
BALLAST BULB

INSIDE HULL:
7,000 POUNDS
TRANSFERABLE WATER
BALLAST

PROLOGUE

FULL BATTENS

LOOSE
FOOT
MAINSAIL

DOGHOUSE

CARBON
FIBER BOOM

TWIN
RUDDERS

ILLUSTRATION BY MARLIN BREE

IT WAS ALL SO PROMISING. He had sailed through hurricanes, dodged icebergs, fought six-story high waves, and even survived a capsizing in 45-foot seas in the Indian Ocean. He was America's most accomplished single-handed offshore sailor and, after three daring circumnavigations, Mike Plant was now starting a fourth voyage with his bold new sailboat.

Coyote was designed to race nonstop and unassisted around the world – a circumnavigation of nearly 24,000 miles in one of the most demanding sea races ever conceived.

At 60 feet in length and flying a cloud of sail atop a huge black mast, *Coyote* was a brute, the most awesome racer Mike had ever attempted to run in the Vendee Globe Challenge. She was Mike's passion; he was gambling everything on her.

Coyote hit the water only weeks before he had to shove off on a late-season run across the North Atlantic. Mike had been a one-man band trying to get her shaken down, put her through sea trials, and get her equipped and provisioned for more than 100 days at sea on the most dangerous oceans of the world.

With only 15 days left, Mike set sail alone out of New York harbor, pressing his new boat hard against the edge of an oncoming storm. He needed to cross the North Atlantic to meet his deadline at Les Sables d'Olonne, France, about 3,200 miles away.

But then the voyage began to go horribly wrong.

From official records and from a reconstruction of possible events, we can build the story of Mike's final voyage.

131

Photo / Billy Black

THE
PASSION
OF
MIKE
PLANT

America's greatest solo sailing hero
takes his final ride in *Coyote*

MIDNIGHT IN THE MIDDLE OF THE NORTH ATLANTIC: *Coyote's* deeply reefed mainsail and sturdy storm jib caught the sudden North Atlantic gust. Spray flashing from her bow, the big racer dug her lee rail in, careening into the wave's dark trough. She picked up speed all the way down.

Mike Plant braced himself against the giant wheel, jubilantly feeling his big racer's power. The boat began to vibrate and shake; the twin rudders' high-speed hum became a high-pitched scream.

From behind the great machine, a rooster tail of water shot skyward. *Coyote's* sharp bow slashed into the oncoming wave, cutting deep. A torrent of ocean rolled back over the deck, slapping Mike in the face.

A thin smile crossed his lips – despite all the odds, despite all the troubles, he was on his way at last across the stormy North Atlantic.

HIS BEAUTY OF A BOAT, *Coyote* was alive in his hands, surging through the heavy seas with speed and vitality. Her sails, hull and rudder all had messages for him. The big boat told him what she felt and what she wanted to do. He was her keeper and she was his best friend.

Tonight on the Gulf Stream, he had almost no visibility. There was danger in the boat's tremendous speed and the oncoming black waves that roared as they got closer and loomed large as islands.

Mike was bone weary, cold and wet.

There was no rest ahead, either. He had to tough it out this raw November night to hand steer because of his boat's electronics failure.

He'd been hand steering his giant racer for eight days.

Because he had no electricity, he had no automatic helm to give him any relief in the storm waters. He had no lights onboard and his navigation system was out.

But he took joy in the fact that *Coyote* was moving well. In his hands, she felt solid and good.

They'd push on – hard. That was their style.

It was the only way to win races.

THE 41-YEAR-OLD SAILOR was bound for Les Sables d'Olonne, France, to enter *Coyote* in the Vendee Globe Challenge single-handed race around the world.

They had left New York October 16 and were gunning to get in under the wire to meet the skipper's deadline of October 31. The 3,200-mile dash across the North Atlantic was his first ocean shakedown alone in his new racer.

He'd use use the run to qualify *Coyote* for the ocean race.

Before the electronics went out, he'd had other problems he thought they'd overcome. During trials, she had run hard aground twice in Chesapeake Bay.

She seemed all right at first, but he had detected a slight vibration somewhere down below from the area at the tip of his radical 14-foot deep keel, with its 8,400-pound lead ballast bulb. It had kept *Coyote* sailing flat out into the teeth of the storm, eating up the miles.

If he just got her across the Big Pond, there'd be plenty of time to haul her and inspect the keel and bulb. His crewmembers, who had flown on ahead of him, were waiting for him.

The shores of France beckoned.

COYOTE caught a blast of cold air and lunged down another wave train.

Mike gritted his teeth, his arms aching.

The big racer heeled precipitously, one of her twin rudders out of the water.

Mike could feel the boat straining and creaking beneath him as every sail, every line, every winch loaded up at maximum pressure.

Twelve...Fourteen knots. He had to estimate the speed. The boat was fantastic!

Suddenly, he felt an odd motion.

The hull vibrated and the deck slammed under his feet.

Mike gripped the wheel. Something was awfully wrong.

In the dark, from below came a low rumble, like that of a freight train.

A sudden shuddering shot through the hull.

Rudder groaning, Mike spun the wheel.

But there was no holding her now.

Coyote canted dangerously, her windward side rearing up, her mast reaching down into the the fury of the waves.

There was a dull cracking noise – and the dark seas rushed up with terrible finality.

Photo / Lucian and Mary Brown

The young racer: Mike with his home-built boat on Lake Minnetonka

MIKE PLANT WAS AN AMERICAN ORIGINAL: he came out of nowhere on the international racing scene and in a few short years stood on the threshold of greatness and fame. He had incredible focus and drive, even before he got into the unique, and uniquely dangerous sport of solo long-distance ocean racing.

He loved adventure. "I think Mike was born with this spirit," his mother, Mary Plant, recalled.

Born in 1950, Mike grew up along the shores of Minnesota's Lake Minnetonka, on the western edge of Minneapolis. "We were fortunate to live very near the Minnetonka Yacht Club," Mary said, "and all the children went to sailing school. Mike was the only one who really took to sailing."

The Plants bought a second-hand X-Boat and Mike would go out many times on his own just to sail around the lake. Mike called his boat, *Lucky Strike.*

"He was very focused, " Mary recalled, "and always working on the boat, changing gear and improving little things." He was a good sailor and by age 12 he was winning races.

"Mike loved challenges," his mother recalled. "As a young boy, he was always thinking of things to do and loved hands-on projects. He built a one-person boat with a motor and he'd scoot around close to shore.

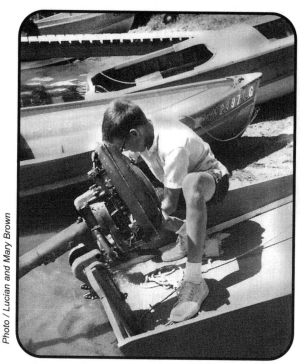

Wearing thick eyeglasses, young Mike Plant tinkers with the outboard engine on his home-built speedboat on Lake Minnetonka.

Photo / Lucian and Mary Brown

He built a small shack near the water's edge where he and a group of neighborhood kids would sell candy and pop. They would round up old boats and fix them up in hopes of selling some.

"Mike was a 'doer,'" Mary said. "The spirit of adventure came as he got older. He was full of action."

But he also had a problem. When Mike was two years old, his mother saw him hold various items up close to his eyes to look at them. Concerned, she took her young son to see an ophthalmologist to have his eyes checked.

"As it turned out, he was very near sighted," Mary said. "He started to wear very thick glasses and was later termed 'legally blind.' In his early teens, he began to wear contact lenses.

I FIRST MET MIKE in Minnetonka, MN, when he was an instructor at Minnesota Outward Bound. By age 18, he had been teaching survival and team building through wilderness adventures programs.

He was making a name for himself as an adventurer and a survival specialist. He hiked from his home in Minnesota down through South America to the tip at Tierra del Fuego, a distance of 12,000 miles, largely on foot.

"How could you do that?" I asked. A lone American, hiking through remote provinces and dangerous jungles, could have been easy prey for bandits and mercenaries.

"I didn't have anything they wanted," he told me.

Mike took naturally to Outward Bound. The organization was conceived in Great Britain during World War II, when many British seamen unaccountably died at sea while awaiting rescue after being torpedoed by German U-boats. The program was designed to instill self-reliance, spiritual tenacity and to develop innate abilities to help seamen survive under difficult conditions.

These were lessons Mike learned, taught others and believed in himself.

After leaving Minnesota-based Outward Bound, boating attracted him once more and he traveled to Lake Superior, where he bought a used 30-foot Cheoy Lee sailboat at Bayfield, WI, near the Apostle Islands. He sailed eastward across Superior, through the Great Lakes, down to New York and out into the North Atlantic to St. Thomas, in the Virgin Islands. Throughout the winter, he lived on his boat in the islands and did some contract work, primarily as a carpenter.

When spring came, he sailed northward with a friend, but neither knew where they wanted to go. His friend suggested they go to Newport for the Newport-to-Bermuda sailboat race. They saw the start of the race and Mike remained in Newport, working as a charter skipper to deliver other boats to ports in the U.S. and the Caribbean. Between assignments, he earned money doing carpentry and house painting.

But in 1983, he told me, he saw a film about an around-the-world sailboat race that "changed my life." It was the 1982 – 83 BOC Challenge, a yacht race for around-the-world solo sailors.

It was an epiphany. Suddenly, he knew what he wanted: be a long-distance sailboat racer.

"When I walked out of the theatre," he explained, "it was like a light switch had gone on. I've never really looked back."

IT WAS A LONG WAY between dreaming about being an ocean racer and actually getting a boat to enter a race. The nautical competition was fierce and the around-the-world sailboat races were dominated by the well-funded European syndicates – especially, the French racing super stars.

Their boats and their skippers seemed unbeatable.

Undeterred, Mike told his mother, "I'm going in the next race."

He began building his first blue-water racing boat on a shoe-string budget in his front yard evenings and weekends, while he worked days as a building contractor. Friends pitched in to help him build a 50-foot water ballasted sloop, working from a new design by Rodger Martin. Mike was the naval architect's first customer.

Somehow, with his home-built boat, Mike hoped to compete against the world's top racers, their multi-million dollar designs, and their well-honed racing programs.

He took his boat to the starting line in Newport in 1986 for the BOC Globe Challenge, in which solo sailors raced their giant sailboats 27,550 miles around the world, with only three stops. As he set off in *Airco Distributor*, all three of his autopilots failed, one by one. That meant he had to hand-steer all the way to the next stop, but Mike kept going. "I'm not going to turn back," he radioed.

Mike's home-built *Airco Distributor* circled the globe in a total elapsed time of 157 days 11 hours and 44 minutes, bettering the previous record by 50 days. He won his class.

THE INTERNATIONAL RACING WORLD took notice. A lone American had become one of the world's most successful single-handed offshore sailors. Moreover, he had done it on his own terms and he had overcome enormous obstacles.

Around the old sailing port of Newport, Mike was no longer another boat bum and dreamer. He was a fire-in-belly skipper, a real racer. And he had only begun to fulfill his dream.

In 1989, the Vendee Globe Challenge was conceived as nothing less than the ultimate ocean racer's race: a challenge to race solo around the world, without stops for rest or reprovisioning. Racers would not be able to get outside help. The brutal, nonstop marathon would run 24,000 miles, west to east, rounding the earth's most dreaded capes, including the fearsome Cape Horn and the misnamed Cape of Good Hope. He'd not only have to survive the horrors of the Southern Ocean, but have to carry sail as long as he could and race across it.

This was truly the ultimate race and it represented a gigantic new challenge. It also meant a new boat for Mike. Again, he turned to his friend, Rodger Martin, for a design to speed him round the world nonstop. And to win a race.

Mike had to dig deeply into his own meager resources to build his boat. In the U.S., he could not get enough sponsors to fund his racing challenge.

He began construction of his 60-foot boat in a rented shed. *Duracell* would have twin rudders, a super-fast hull and state-of-the-art water ballast. Mike sailed the boat across the North Atlantic to France to qualify and after the race began, soon became the early leader, despite suffering for a week from a virus infection. He toughed it out and got well at sea while he raced.

In the Pacific Ocean, disaster struck: a $5 part broke on the rigging. Mike had to sail 36 hours straight until he was able to anchor off Campbell Island, New Zealand. A storm caught him and began pushing the racer toward a rocky shore's certain destruction.

On the island, four meteorologists saw the racer's plight and motored out in their Zodiac. To save his boat with its dragging anchor, Mike had to accept the tow, but he knew that the outside assistance would disqualify him.

The meteorologists suggested to Mike that he simply continue the race. They vowed eternal silence. No one would know.

"Except I would," Mike answered.

Mike radioed the race committee that he had accepted outside help and that he would continue the race, though disqualified. He unofficially crossed the finish line in seventh place.

Mike lost the race, but to the admiring French, he emerged a real hero. His determination and honesty did not go unnoticed: 25,000 people lined the breakwater in Les Sables d'Olonne to give him a rousing hero's welcome. Mike was the only American in the race.

Herb McCormick, editor of *Cruising World*, and the Boating Editor of the *New York Times* wrote: "The tens of thousands of French men and women who greeted him at the finish understood something that largely was missed in this country. By forging on, by completing what he'd set out to do, by showing the highest respect for his competitors in a wonderful act of sportsmanship, Mike was as much a winner as the sailors who'd officially crossed the finish line."

Despite delays, Mike set the American record for the shortest time to circumnavigate the world single-handed. He did it in 134 days.

IN 1990, HE ENTERED AN UPGRADED AND MODIFIED *DURACELL* in the BOC Challenge, again setting sail from Newport. His effort caught the attention of Minnesota Senator David Durenberger, who read a section of a *New York Times* report into the *Congressional Record.* He noted that Mike was the only American in the single-handed, around-the-world, nonstop yacht race that was regarded by sailors as "the ultimate test of courage, stamina and resourcefulness."

As *Duracell* neared Cape Town, South Africa, in the 6,800 mile first leg of the race, Sen. Durenberger read into the *Record:* "After 35 days on the open seas, fatigue has become Mike's constant companion. Mike has slept in his bunk only twice during the trip. His daily sleeping routine is to work and sleep in 20-minute intervals...Hundreds of miles from the nearest shore, Mike is now running low on food. Most of his remaining food supply exists in the form of carbohydrates and starches, namely beans and rice. But Mike and the *Duracell* are likely to overcome their obstacles and regain lost ground during the next two legs of the race. It is in these two legs that the winds above the southern seas are stronger than in any other part of the race. As Mike traverses through the turbulent seas below the equator, the spirit of Minnesota will go with him.

"Mike thrives on the inter-relationship with nature that solo, offshore sailboat racing provides. He once said that offshore sailboat racing 'strips you to the soul– exposing who we are, what we are (and) why we exist.' To Minnesotans and Americans alike, Mike's courage, leadership, and the ability to overcome adversity symbolizes who we are, what we are, and why we exist. His spirit of competition and determination serves as a beacon of goodwill from Minnesota to the world."

In Capetown, South Africa, a competitor collided with his boat, but Mike repaired *Duracell's* bow while continuing to race.

He made it around the world in 132 days 20 hours, bettering his previous time by two days – and won a new U.S. record for solo circumnavigation.

H E WAS NOW AMERICA'S PREMIERE single-handed sailor and he had come out of nowhere in only six years. In France, he got the nickname of "Top Gun" for his passion for carrying sail in heavy seas and wild winds.

It seemed that there was little Mike couldn't do or survive. A certain mystique surrounded him. He had savvy, capability, and endurance, honed on the oceans of the world. He came to love the solitude and the challenge of single-handed, long-distance sailing. He was happiest when he was alone at sea with his boat.

When family and sailing friends didn't hear from him, they knew it was because he was into "his racing mode." They'd hear from him when the race was over. He was passionate about his boat, his race, and his dream.

But the challenge was getting harder. To compete in the 1992-93 Vendee Globe Challenge, Mike would need as powerful a boat as he could get to keep up with the aggressive, and better-funded, French racers. The boat had to be strong and above all, it had to be fast.

Once again he turned to Rodger Martin to design a breakthrough boat, a racer ahead of its time. Mike knew what he wanted and he had more than a handful of ideas.

Another around-the-world sailor, Dodge Morgan, who was the first American to sail alone nonstop around the world, had an ominous viewpoint: "Mike had a boat designed close to the edge and built perhaps a little closer," he was quoted as saying in news stories. He added, "Mike knew what he was doing and so did the people who worked with him. They wanted to win a race."

C OYOTE WAS DESIGNED TO BE A FLAT-OUT SUPER BOAT, a high-performance ocean dragster powered by a huge sail area and a knife-blade keel, designed to do only one thing: rip around the world single-handed at top speed and to win the Vendee Globe Race.

At 60-foot overall, *Coyote* was a skimmer that could soar over the waves, rather than plow through them. With a menacing plumb bow, flat transom, and straight sheerline, she projected brute force. "Beautiful, but with a raw, brutal type of beauty," *Coyote's* sail maker, Dan Neri, described her.

But for other sailors, *Coyote* looked like a "monstrous boat." "That thing is an animal," one man said, pointing out, "that boat could be difficult to handle with a crew of *ten* on board."

She was beamy for a sailboat at nearly 19 feet 4 inches in width and flat on the deck, like an "aircraft carrier," as her naval architect sometimes joked. She had a low freeboard, which meant she had little wind resistance, but that also would make her a wet boat. She could catch and fling back the waves she couldn't fly over. Incredibly, *Coyote's* 60-foot hull itself only drew 1 foot 3 inches of water.

Inside, you had to squat to move around, for she only had 4 feet of headroom, except in the small doghouse, which had a headroom of 6 feet.

Mike was a fanatic on lightness, since less weight to drag around equated to a faster boat. With her E-glass set in epoxy over foam-core construction, *Coyote* was a strong but ultra-light-weight flyer. She would displace only 21,500 pounds, nearly 6,000 pounds lighter than *Duracell,* which had an approximate average speed of 11 knots.

Coyote would also set approximately 50 percent more sail area than *Duracell*, a small cloud of 2,935 square feet of sail (based on a forward headsail of 1305 square feet and full mainsail), on her 85-foot carbon fiber mast. Her main alone was 1,630 square feet and it weighed 250 pounds. This sail took a lot of muscle and stamina to raise and handle, even on a 2- to-1 halyard and a pow-erful winch. To raise the mainsail from the boom to the top of the mast would take Mike about 10 minutes of hard work. Her largest spinnaker was 2,800 square feet.

Like most of her class of ocean racers, she had a very long fore triangle with her mast set back at more than 50 percent of the waterline, so that she could carry an effective inner forestay. Dan Neri explained, "It is not practical to change headsails with one man on a boat that big, so they use a reaching/light wind headsail on the forward stay and a heavy air jib on the inner stay." Both foresails were set on furlers, with controls leading back to the cockpit.

Her mast was hollow, built of braided carbon fiber and glass, and very light at about 3 pounds per foot for its 85-foot tall height. With its advanced triple-spreader design, it was thin and flexible and would need attention to keep it properly tuned and in column. But it would be fast.

To carry that much power in her sails, *Coyote* had a 14-foot deep "knife blade" keel for minimum resistance while ripping through the world's oceans. At 40 inches in length and 6 inches in thickness, the keel was strongly built with 42 layers of Kevlar and carbon fiber. The carbon fiber fin encapsulated a heavy stainless steel plate at its bottom, to which the bulb was bolted. Six heavy stainless steel bolts extended through the plate and the bulb, and were secured with nuts. The whole unit was overlapped with 15 layers of carbon fiber for extra strength.

At the bottom hung a torpedo-shaped lead bulb that weighed 8,400 pounds. It was 112 inches long, 18 inches high and 27 inches wide.

Coyote also could carry an extra 7,000 pounds of transferable water ballast in two tanks, so she could get extra weight on the windward side to keep her level on a wild reach. For safety, she had 5 air-tight compartments for floatation and she was designed and built as strong as possible, with special attention to impact strength. With her Airex foam core hull, she would have enough inherent floatation to remain afloat even if she was holed and her hull flooded with water.

Mike's *Coyote* would be the most extreme 60-foot monohull ever launched in the U.S., the ultimate weapon to race nonstop around the world.

"*Coyote* met and surpassed her advance advertisements," wrote Herb McCormick. "She was the fastest, wildest, wettest monohull that I have ever sailed."

WHEN I MET HIM AT THE MINNEAPOLIS BOAT SHOW, Mike told me that funds were very slow in coming in. He was not a wealthy man and he hoped to rely on sponsors and other financial help to get his racer built. Financing the boat was a big concern: big, custom racers like *Coyote* could cost a whopping $650,000 to $800,000, and sometimes more, a lot more, depending upon what exotic materials you wanted to put into them. To race successfully, you couldn't scrimp. You needed the exotics.

He talked about doing a book with me, but that project faded when we discussed the time required to write and to publish a manuscript. Mike just didn't have the time.

He was faced with a multitude of construction details on the custom-racer being built at Concordia Custom Yachts, of South Dartmouth, Mass. He was not a sailor to place an order with a yard and then show up when the boat was ready. It was his racer, and from his extensive racing experience, he had specific things in mind.

"Mike knew what he wanted and he had a great understanding of what the boat would be put through," Dan Neri said. Dan went with Mike to the boatyard several times when the boat was being built. "Mike was deeply involved in the decision making for the assembly of the structural parts of the boat," he said. "Some of those decisions were made on the fly, to the point where Mike was drawing on scraps of plywood to illustrate his ideas."

The boat was in a "slow-build" program: the yard started it, and built it, on and off, as Mike came up with money. "Mike was a hands-on man in everything he did," Dan said. "He was trying to manage the boat build, mast engineering and construction, sail inventory planning, electronics installation, fund raising and preparations for sea trials and ultimately his campaign for the Vendee Globe. He had a charisma that drew people to his cause and there was a small army of people in Rhode Island doing what we could to help him out. I am sure many of us have thought we should have pulled him aside and tried to talk him into slowing down."

But that was not to be. "With Mike there was no indecision," Dan said. "Everything was about meeting the next goal."

Coyote was intended to be a high-tech, custom-built dreamboat racer using the best of everything new. Dan said, "Mike brought together his team of friends and associates and this very state-of- the-art race boat was built by craftsmen relying on their best instincts and experience." He added, "In some areas, the design was beyond that experience base."

"The team at Concordia were among the best in the business,"

Dan said. "If any group could pull off this build project, it was these guys, and at the time, a seat of the pants approach to high-tech yacht building was not so unusual. But looking back on it, we were clearly pushing too close to the limits of the materials."

Instead of an early 1992 launch, followed by leisurely sea trials in fair weather on the North Atlantic, the boat came off the ramps September 10 – six months behind Mike's original schedule. The critical keel to bulb assembly was completed only days before launch date.

He had only 7 weeks to get the boat ready and to be in France for the race.

T HE POWER OF *COYOTE* WAS PHENOMENAL. She accelerated quickly and on a reach she tore across the water like no other boat Mike had ever sailed. Her cruising speed was calculated at 18 knots – practically flying.

But as Dan Neri pointed out, "there are considerations for handling an extreme boat like this." At 60 feet in length, *Coyote* was no sailing dinghy and Dan said, "you plan about 4 steps in advance, but focus on the next step at all times."

Because *Coyote* had no engine, the big boat was towed by an inflatable powerboat when docking or departing. Getting her underway was a little difficult, though, because the mast was fairly far aft. "The boat actually wanted to sail backwards with just the mainsail up," Dan said. "For that reason it was important to keep it going forward at all times, no different than most big boats."

With Dan aboard, Mike tested *Coyote* off Newport in Rhode Island Sound.

"My most vivid memories are of looking up the rig while fetching in 25 knots of wind and the boat crashing along at 11 knots," Dan said. "The mast lacked torsional stiffness for some reason. Either the tube did not have enough off-axis wraps, the spreader geometry was wrong, or it did not have enough shroud tension. The mast moved more than any rig I had seen before or since. The mast was built in 4 sections, which were joined at the boat shop. Mike had a set of alloy spreaders that I think were supposed to be used for the mold to make carbon spreaders, but they were used on the mast instead. So it was a big, high load spar system built, again, by a group of excellent composite boat builders, but without the benefit of the level of engineering we are accustomed to today."

Dan recalls that *Coyote* was "incredibly loud inside" when sailing with the breeze forward of the beam. "It was also very loud off the wind, but the off-the-wind noises were not as alarming," Dan said. He later explained: "Today, we are used to the noise, but with *Coyote* being the first of its type, the noise was new and a little unnerving.

"The best day of sailing was during a photo shoot off the mouth of the Sackonett River," Dan recalls. "There were long ocean swells from a low pressure system well offshore and a 20-knot sea breeze. We had a kite up, surfing in the high teens, and, all of the crew inside the boat so the helicopter could film Mike sailing it alone. Davis Murray, Mike's buddy from the Virgin Islands, was steering with the autopilot while looking out the windows. As a joke, Davis made the boat bear off at the bottom of a trough while Mike was standing on the bow in the hero pose with one hand on the head stay. The bow dug in and the wave caromed back along the foredeck and slammed across the window. When the water cleared, Mike was standing there, drenched and smiling. We did it again. This time, Mike held on to the head stay with both hands and let the wave pick him up so that his whole body was streaming aft, parallel with the deck."

Crew high-jinks aside, *Coyote* was proving herself as a remarkable boat.

"*Coyote* tracked quite well," Dan said. "All of Rodger's boats sail great off the wind. The heeled water plane is close to symmetrical so the boat wants to go in a straight line. There is actually plenty of keel area and it is efficient so there is always attached flow. The leeward rudder is vertical, or both are working at lower heel angles. The rudders are balanced so there are fewer loads on the autopilots. The boat was much more kind on the pilots than more 'conventional' boats that become less balanced with heel. The boat could be sailed for days at a time under autopilot. Obviously the sail plan has to be set up correctly. If the boat is overpowered it will behave badly.

"Compared to a heavy displacement boat, I would say that *Coyote* felt like she was on rails most of the time. The boat was very fast and with speed you get directional stability. The flip side is that if the autopilot wanders too far, a fast boat can take a quick turn toward the wind. Steering problems are usually a function of the sail trim and pilot setup rather than the boat design."

As they tested the big boat, Mike discovered a few problems. As Dan relates: "*Coyote* did not go to weather as well as a typical fully crewed race boat. The hull shape is optimized for reaching and running. In a long distance ocean race, the only times you want to be hard on the wind is when you have to while leaving harbors and approaching harbors. Otherwise, you sail a slightly more freed-up angle toward a more favorable part of the weather system, or the next weather system."

Mary Plant minced no words. When going to weather, she said, "of all the boats Mike had, *Coyote* was the most miserable."

Mike and his crew discovered during sea trials that when *Coyote* reached a speed of about 9 knots, the keel's foil and bulb began to create a humming sound. The crew checked out the keel through the sight glass – a piece of Plexiglas through the hull to see the keel while the vessel was underway – but they couldn't see any problem. In addition to the noise, they felt a vibration coming from the keel. As *Coyote's* speed increased, the sound and the vibrations would change. Mike dismissed the noise and vibrations as problems common to racers like *Coyote.*

Overall, Mike was happy. His new racer performed brilliantly and he worked hard to learn her special ways. But the harder he worked, the further he seemed to fall behind.

Mike was a list keeper and at one time, he said that the he had a million things left to do before he left. He confided to a friend that his list was "so long now, I've lost the beginning of it."

S AILING TO ANNAPOLIS, *Coyote* continued to reveal her potential. Spreading her wings on the North Atlantic, the big racer averaged 16 knots and during one stretch, she reached a sustained speed of 24 knots. Mike was elated.

But in Chesapeake Bay, *Coyote* ran into trouble.

Under sail at 9:30 a.m., *Coyote* was east of the entrance to Annapolis harbor on a reach and hitting upwards of 9 knots with a jib up and a reef in her main. "

These were perfect conditions for what Mike had in mind,"

photographer Billy Black recalled. "Flat water, good wind."

Billy was at the wheel when *Coyote's* deep keel abruptly plowed into the bottom and a soft thud echoed through the hull. The big sailboat's bow did a little dip, and she slid to a stop. "It was a soft, gentle landing," Billy recalls. "We just settled in."

She had run aground, burying her 14-foot deep bulb into the bottom mud estimated at 12 to 13 feet below. In the 12-knot wind out of the north, *Coyote* started to cant sideways under the pressure of her sails, tugging on her keel.

A CCORDING TO A COAST GUARD REPORT, the following sequence of events transpired: Mike first tried to sail her off, and succeeded in heeling the big sailboat over and turning her about 180 degrees, but this maneuver did not dislodge the ballast bulb. She remained aground.

As 20-foot fishing boat passed by, Mike hailed it for help. To get more leverage to get the bulb out of the muck, they passed *Coyote's* halyard to her mast top over to the powerboat. The obliging skipper gave the throttle some gas and *Coyote's* mast top took up the strain. Below the water, the ballast bulb remained firmly wedged. That wasn't working, so the boat backed up and the big sailboat came upright again.

A quick conference and it was time for another try. Mike passed a towing line aft of the bow and another line to the stern. The powerboat throttled up and slowly, *Coyote's* long hull canted sideways and the buried bulb popped loose.

At the dock in Annapolis, Mike and his crew took turns looking down the sight glass at the keel. No one noticed anything abnormal.

"Mike took it in stride," Billy said. "No problems."

Later, as they sailed out of Annapolis, *Coyote* once again went aground in the bay. This time, two workboats took the big boat in tow and yanked her off the bottom.

Mike wondered whether he should take *Coyote* to a boat yard, hoist her out of the water and inspect for damage. The two groundings could have put shock loads and stresses on the keel and the fasteners that held on the ballast bulb.

But there was no time.

The North Atlantic – and the big race – awaited.

I N NEW YORK HARBOR, *Coyote* made a triumphant debut. She looked sleek and able, a beautiful racer eager to do battle with the dark waters of the world.

With Mike at the helm, *Coyote* slipped along, a lithe young animal quick to respond under the reduced sail of a reefed main and a small jib. Even a little sail was enough to move the boat along smartly.

The schedule was tight, but Mike planned to sail out of New York on Friday, Oct.16, and arrive October 30 in Les Sables d'Olonne, France, 3,200 miles away. A two-week passage across the North Atlantic would be remarkably quick, but *Coyote* was a fast boat and Mike had been across "the Big Pond" a number of times. He knew how to drive his big boat hard, if he needed to.

Departure day was sunny but ominously breezy, with a powerful wind out of the southeast. Various well-wishers stopped by to bid Mike a swift voyage, including famed America's Cup sailor Dennis Connors, who walked over to give Mike a copy of his latest book. "Maybe this will help you," Dennis had joked. Mike enjoyed a good laugh: Dennis' new book was about how to sail.

Al Roker from NBC's *Today Show* interviewed Mike. Millions of viewers saw the young Minnesota sailor about to depart on his globe-girdling quest in his new racer. The TV program planned to have a satellite broadcast with Mike during the race.

Then it was time to go. Under a powerboat's tow, *Coyote* gracefully moved into the harbor and past the historic windjammers at the South Street Seaport Museum. Mike gathered up fenders, cast off *Coyote's* towline and raised the sails.

Free in the rising southeast wind, the big racer came to life. A cloud of canvas tightened, then grew taut as the great boat heeled and gracefully flew out of the harbor, eager for its first crossing.

Everyone stood in awe watching Mike and *Coyote* loping off into the distance to the awaiting North Atlantic.

"He looked straight ahead," a spectator said. "He never looked back."

L ATE IN THE SEASON, the North Atlantic was changing. Always potentially dangerous, the big ocean could turn into a nightmare of gale force winds, bitter cold and broken seas as winter came on.

By his third day, the wind was blowing on the nose at 35 knots, and Mike was having trouble steering in heavy seas.

In a radio-telephone message to a friend, he called the storm, "god-awful."

As a veteran of numerous North Atlantic crossings, he expected that he'd encounter rough conditions. But he had never anticipated the stomach-churning jolts and crashes as his new extreme racer speared waves and scooped water over the deck.

He was in the Gulf Stream, where the Labrador current becomes a virtual river of water running toward the east that should have given him an easy lift of several knots per hour toward France. But the storm was out of the east and winds were blowing *against* the fast-moving stream, piling it into big haystacks of waves.

Coyote would fly down the backside of one wave and partly bury her bow in the oncoming wave. Then her bow would yank up, she'd fling back a fire-hose spray and water over her deck, and, she'd climb over the wave. It was a brutal, abrupt motion, punishing to boat and man.

Mike reported that he was having trouble steering in the heavy seas and that the boat was laboring as he struggled to hold *Coyote's* bow close to the wind.

Going upwind was *Coyote's* worst point of sail: she was designed to be a downwind flyer. With her relatively flat bottom, razor keel and extreme light displacement, she pounded into the waves at relatively high speeds. It all added up to a bruising, miserable ride.

Coyote's big main was deeply reefed and Mike had only a storm jib hanked on the inner forestay, but even this patch of sail seemed at times too much to offer up to the gods of the storm. Mike braced himself behind the big wheel, trying to summon up all the reserves of strength and energy he had learned to horde.

He drove her hard, for she did not point high and needed speed to cover distance. His deadline loomed.

If the North Atlantic were rough, he and *Coyote* would have to be rougher. He had faith they could do it.

WITH HIS SAT PHONE, Mike called his friends and crew to keep them informed of his progress. He called on Friday, Oct. 16, Saturday, Oct. 17, and, 6 times on Sunday, Oct. 18. By that time, he'd slowed the boat down to about 12 knots so he could sort things out. He also was feeling optimistic and in a good mood.

But Mike made no more radio contacts until Wednesday, October 21, when he used a hand-held VHF radio to contact a passing freighter, the *SKS Trader.*

He was about a third of the way across the Atlantic, 940 miles from New York, and some 1,300 miles from the area where *Coyote* would eventually be located.

"I have no power, but I'm working on the problem," Mike reported to the freighter's captain, adding that he had been working on the electrical system for 3 days. He planned to have the problem solved by morning.

It turned out that on Oct. 19, he had lost not only his radios but *all* of his electrical power. He kept going.

WITHOUT HIS ELECTRICAL SYSTEMS, Mike had serious problems. Not only had he lost his regular radios – and could not send out an SOS, for example, if he ran into trouble, nor could he get the all-important weather reports – but he no longer had electricity to power his auto pilots. That meant he had to hand steer *Coyote* to keep his boat moving.

He had to watch her carefully, for she was just too slippery a racer to let fly along by herself unattended for any long periods of time. In these stormy conditions and waves, he couldn't lash the wheel and go below to have a proper night's sleep. He could only catnap at the wheel.

Adding to his worries was the matter of *Coyote's* insurance coverage. Mike had applied for insurance for *Coyote* before he left New York Harbor, but he had not received confirmation that his boat was insured before he left.

Now at sea, the possibility of his boat not being covered by insurance added to his worries. If something happened to his boat, or if he lost his boat at sea, he'd be in dire financial straits.

In fact, he'd nearly be ruined financially.

BELOW DECKS, the racer was a maze of vibrations and movement as she sliced through the waves. Her hull was alive with the noises of her passage through the heavy water and she seemed

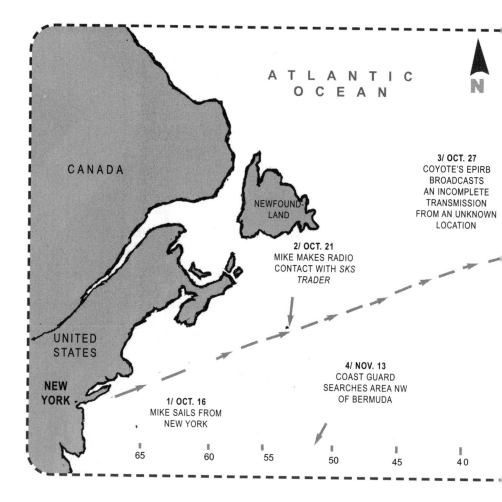

1/ Friday, Oct. 16: Mike Plant sails *Coyote* from New York City for Les Sables, d'Olonne, France. He intends a quick crossing to arrive in time for the start Oct. 31 of the Vendee Globe Race in Les Sables-d'Olonne, France.

2/ Wednesday, Oct. 21: Mike radios from tanker *SKS Trader* and reports he has lost all electrical power. He has had to hand steer for the past 3 days.

3/ Tuesday, October 27, near midnight, *Coyote's* EPIRB sends an incomplete emergency beacon. It is believed that this was the date of *Coyote's* capsize.

Friday, Oct. 30: Intended date of arrival of *Coyote* in France.

Friday Nov. 6: *Coyote i*s overdue in France and the U.S. Coast Guard sends out an alert for all ships at sea.

Tuesday, Nov. 10: The French Coast Guard is asked to initiate a search for the missing vessel, but the request is declined.

Wednesday, Nov. 11: Frank and Mary Plant request that the U.S. Coast Guard conduct a search. This request is turned down because of insufficient information about approximate location for a search.

4/ Friday, Nov. 13: The Coast Guard begins to search in an area NW of Bermuda on coordinates supplied by Canadian Mission Control.

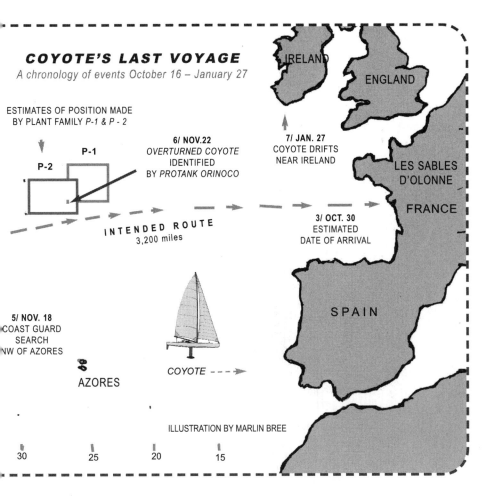

COYOTE'S LAST VOYAGE

A chronology of events October 16 – January 27

ESTIMATES OF POSITION MADE
BY PLANT FAMILY *P-1 & P - 2*

P-1

P-2

6/ NOV.22
OVERTURNED COYOTE
IDENTIFIED
BY *PROTANK ORINOCO*

7/ JAN. 27
COYOTE DRIFTS
NEAR IRELAND

IRELAND

ENGLAND

LES SABLES
D'OLONNE

FRANCE

3/ OCT. 30
ESTIMATED
DATE OF ARRIVAL

INTENDED ROUTE
3,200 miles

5/ NOV. 18
COAST GUARD
SEARCH
NW OF AZORES

AZORES

COYOTE - - - ►

SPAIN

ILLUSTRATION BY MARLIN BREE

30   25   20   15

5/ Wednesday, Nov. 18: The Coast Guard extends its search area to include an area north of Azores

Thursday, Nov. 19: The Coast Guard suspends search

Friday, Nov. 20: The Coast Guard searches in a new area north of Azores when weather improves.

6/ Sunday, Nov. 22: The overturned hull of *Coyote* is discovered by *Protank Orinoco* at 46 -54 N, 26 -51 W. British Nimrod aircraft conduct a flare search.

Wednesday, Nov. 25: French tug *Malabar* arrives alongside *Coyote* and divers search underneath the hull.

7/ Wed. Jan. 27: *Coyote* drifts to approximately 70 miles south and west of the coast of Ireland and is towed to shore.

Note: During the search, the Plant family attempted to estimate the position of *Coyote* based on calculations of wind and waves (See squares P - 1 and P - 2). The overturned hull of the lost racer was found eventually in P - 2 by the tanker *Protank Orinoco*

to boom when she fell off a large wave. At above 9 knots, the keel made its humming sound and began to vibrate. Going down a wave's back, when *Coyote* picked up speed, the keel vibrated and hummed more.

There was little comfort below decks, since *Coyote* was stripped out for speed. The interior of the boat was outfitted with a minimum of amenities and equipment: a chart table, with computers and navigational equipment, some shelves and a stove to heat up some food. There were stacks of food and provisions everywhere. He'd have time to sort things out better in France after he met his deadline.

The electrical system had worked OK during the brief shakedown cruise to Annapolis, but had failed at sea. Actually, *Coyote* had 2 electrical systems: a 12- volt and also a 24-volt. In theory, the 24-volt system would run his autopilots better and faster, a big advantage for steering a fast-moving ocean greyhound like *Coyote*. But it also meant that Mike had to deal with dual voltage systems and the related gear to power them, including generators, relays, regulators and wiring. Whatever the problem was, *Coyote's* power was out.

Mike ended his communication to the freighter by asking the crew to relay a message to his fiancée, Helen Davis. He told her that although *Coyote* had a power failure, he was continuing on to France; that he would probably be delayed in arriving and that she should not worry about him.

It was to be Mike's last message.

OCTOBER IS HURRICANE SEASON on the North Atlantic and another storm with high winds and heavy seas erupted to the north of *Coyote's* route. The hurricane, though worrisome, should not have been a crisis for a high-tech craft like *Coyote*. Mike himself had been through hurricanes before and had been around the world three times in all weather conditions. He had heavy weather experience and he was a resourceful seaman.

But after the radio message with the freighter, Mike did not made another contact. Mike's family and friends grew concerned. Apparently, he still had not been able to fix his electronics problems.

Shortly before midnight on October 27, Mike's EPIRB

(Emergency Position Indicating Radio Beacon) went off and sent a distress burst transmission. Both NOAA (National Oceanic and Atmospheric Agency) and CMC (Canadian Mission Control Center) reported receiving a short, weak, and, incomplete EPIRB signal. NOAA received 2 short bursts at 2321 GMT and the Canadian tracking station picked up 3 transmissions from the same satellite.

The signal was incomplete and not long enough to obtain an accurate fix on the EPIRB's location. When the agencies ran a check on the registration for the hexadecimal code, they found that the signaling unit was not registered by its owner. Neither agency passed the distress signal on to the U.S. Coast Guard. Apparently, Mike had not completed his EPIRB registration information, so the agencies knew a brief signal had been sent, but they did not know who sent it. Or why.

They only knew that someone, or something, had set it off.

By Friday, Oct. 30, Mike had not arrived at the docks in Les Sables d'Olonne, France, and the people waiting for him became worried. Not only hadn't Mike arrived at the time he said he would, but he had been out of touch since Oct. 21.

On Friday, Nov. 6, Concordia Custom Yachts wrote and telephoned the U.S. Coast Guard to tell them that *Coyote* was a week overdue in France. It requested that all ships at sea be on the alert for the missing sailor and gave *Coyote's* emergency radio beacon (EPIRB) number and life raft identification.

On Tuesday, Nov. 10, Mike's crew, waiting for him in Les Sables d'Olonne, turned to the French Coast Guard and requested they initiate a search for the missing *Coyote*. The French turned the request down, stating they said they first needed a formal request from the U.S. Coast Guard.

On Wednesday, Nov. 11, Mike's parents, Mary and Frank Plant, requested a search for their missing son, but the U.S. Coast Guard declined the request because they said they had insufficient information about where to search.

On Thursday, Nov. 12, a friend of Mike's took the initiative and talked to NOAA directly to check if any signal had been received from *Coyote's* EPIRB. Alarmingly, he found that an incomplete signal had been recorded on Oct. 27 – though nothing had been done with the information. The signal, received the evening of Oct. 27 by a Canadian tracking station, consisted of 3 weak transmission bursts from Mike's EPIRB. NOAA had received 2 bursts.

Technically, both agencies required a longer signal of 4 bursts for an accurate location. They had received only 3 bursts and no more. This was strange, since in an emergency situation, an EPIRB should continuously broadcast its location for many hours. They did not have a record of whose EPIRB was broadcasting, since Mike apparently had not registered his unit at the time of purchase or immediately afterward. Or, the registration card had not gotten to the right office.

On Friday, Nov. 13, the U.S. Coast Guard issued an alert for all passing ships to be on the lookout for the missing boat and they began a search covering an area northwest of Bermuda, on coordinates supplied by Canadian Mission Control, of 36-21 N and 52-45W, positioning Mike hundreds of miles south of his intended course.

On Nov. 18, the search was revised and extended to include an area north of the Azores. The searchers found nothing.

A day later, the search was called off.

I N THE MEANTIME, a volunteer group, The Friends of Mike Plant, began lobbying their senators, congressmen and other elected officials to press for an additional search for the missing sailor. Our mission was to get the Coast Guard to resume its search for Mike and *Coyote*.

A member of the Friends, Capt. Thom Burns at *Northern Breezes Sailing Magazine*, sent a letter to the Commandant, United States Coast Guard, urging that the active air search not be suspended or cancelled, because the Coast Guard "has covered approximately one half of the total area its own computers recommended be saturated."

Why had the Coast Guard suspended the active air search with so much area yet to be covered? Capt. Thom asked, pointing out that the search was "too narrow" and that "sailing experts have predicted possible drift patterns well outside the current parameters." He urged that the Coast Guard continue to make "a realistic, moral effort."

Later, Capt. Thom said that "the search needs to be visual

instead of electronic." He explained that the Coast Guard had been flying out to search for Mike using radar and sighting along a path 30 miles wide but "the problem is that at that speed and altitude you can't see something as small as a life raft. And radar is virtually useless picking up a life raft, unless there's a massive radar reflector on it."

The former naval officer said that the 17-day delay in responding to an emergency beacon created a massive problem. "Delaying expands the search areas from 50,000 square miles to 900,000 square miles. And every day it gets bigger." In a separate correspondence, he also urged the Coast Guard to ask the Navy for help, since the Navy flies submarine surveillance training missions out of Brunswick Naval Air Station in Maine.

The Navy authorized two P-3 Orion planes to join the search with infrared sensors that could detect heat in the water. The planes flew out of New Brunswick, Maine, joining 4 Coast Guard C-130 search planes from North Carolina and Florida.

The Plant family and some of Mike's friends brought in meteorologists and navigation experts to try to determine Mike's probable location, based on winds, his speed, and, weather conditions on the North Atlantic. They pinpointed an area well east of the original search area and north of the Azores.

On November 20, the Coast Guard resumed its search of an area north of the Azores. Aircraft and ships from four nations looked for Mike in an search area that eventually covered more than 215,000 square miles of open ocean. It was one of the broadest rescue missions ever in the North Atlantic and eventually involved aircraft and vessels from the U.S. Coast Guard, U.S. Navy, Canada, Great Britain and France.

O N SUNDAY MORNING, NOV. 22, the 750-foot long Greek tanker *Protank Orinocco* saw something dark lying low in the water, drifting upside down. At first the crew did not know what they had found because its dark bottom was awash in 8 to 12-foot waves.

Altering course to steer closer, the tanker captain saw that it was a capsized sailboat whose hull was intact, with twin rudders still upright and a thin keel that pointed heavenward.

In heavy seas and rain, the tanker came within 50 feet and cautiously circled the upside-down hull, scanning the boat with binoculars, looking for any sign of life. They saw none, but they noted that part of the vessel's keel, the ballast bulb, was missing.

Because of the heavy sea conditions, the tanker could not come close or send a boat to board the upturned hull, but they recorded her position and reported them. The coordinates were 46-54 N, 26-51W, which placed the lost vessel about 1,100 nautical miles due West of Les Sables d-Olonne, France, and, about 500 nautical miles north of the Azores.

They waited. Even in heavy seas, they knew that the sound of the tanker's big engines and thrashing propeller alongside the hull would throb loudly through the water, alerting anyone inside. No one appeared from the overturned hull nor gave any signal that they could determine. Slowly, the tanker turned and resumed course.

Later that day, two Coast Guard C-130s and a Navy P-3 Orion as well as a French navy patrol craft searched near the sightings. A British aircraft flew over the lost boat and conducted a flare search in the vicinity of the hull, but they located nothing in the water, such as a life raft or wreckage.

Still hope remained. Sailors worldwide felt that Mike had a fighting chance of being rescued alive if either he went aboard his life raft or was able to survive inside *Coyote's* upturned hull, which was riding high in the water. The latter theory was particularly hopeful since other racers had lived for days inside their overturned but intact hulls.

Three days later, on the morning of Wednesday, Nov. 25, the French tugboat, *Malabar*, arrived alongside the overturned sailboat and positively identified that the hull was the missing racer, *Coyote*. French frogmen dove under the vessel and came up inside the hull, shining their lights about as they searched carefully through the watertight compartments. The hull floated high in the water and they found air pockets where a man could breathe. They located the life raft opened in the cockpit, but uninflated. The CO_2 bottle had not been fired. A survival bag was attached to the raft, and nearby, an unopened bag of distress flares. They found a life jacket tied to a bunk and they also found the partial remains of a torn survival suit − but no sign of the missing sailor.

Because they had found the life raft and survival gear, but no one aboard the overturned hull, the searchers concluded that the lone sailor was no longer alive, for "there are no other possibilities." They left and *Coyote* remained capsized and adrift at sea.

IN THE FADING LIGHT OF A LATE NOVEMBER AFTERNOON, I drove to Lake Minnetonka's old Lafayette Club, located near the beloved waters that Mike had sailed as a boy. In the parking lot were some Mercedes, BMW's, a Lincoln Town car or two and some old, rusty vans. I stepped out into the chilling wind off the lake and walked into the wood frame building.

A number of people had come to pay their respects to America's world-class sailor. Although his body was never recovered, Mike was lost and presumed dead on the North Atlantic. His devoted family had planned for about 300 people, but an overflow crowd of nearly 600 had turned up to honor him.

In the wooden hall, I slipped into a seat and the service began. John Simmons, Mike's nephew, had written a poem, which Mike's brother, Tom, read:

> *Deep Ocean blue is all you will see.*
> *For the rest of time you will have the satisfaction of what you love.*
> *Free as a dove*
> *This is what you love...*
> *This is what you love.*
>
> *...So rest in peace..*
> *Rest in peace in your deep heavenly blue.*
> *We all hope to see you..so someday*
> *Spirit and soul, visit us, we love you.*

The speakers, one by one, got up to talk about the young sailor's life. Mark Schrader, a fellow long-distance racer, recalled that during an around-the-world race in the Southern Ocean, when he was cold, wet and very tired one long night, he talked with Mike on the radio, voicing his fears that his boat was too slow and heavy. Mike was racing just ahead of him.

"Your boat is not too heavy. Your boat is not too slow," Mike responded. Schrader said the admonition was what he needed to continue racing and finished his race.

Schrader admired Mike's calm professionalism: "He sailed the world as though he were sailing across the lake."

Rodger Martin, *Coyote's* designer, talked about his work with Mike and his admiration of Mike's remarkable concentration and determination. The tall naval architect recalled driving by a boatyard when it was closed for a winter holiday. In the icy yard, he was astonished to see Mike Plant all alone working the boatyard's travel lift, slowly lowering his boat onto its awaiting keel.

Surprised by the visitor, Mike turned – and fell down. He had been concentrating on his work so much and for so long that his shoes had frozen to the ground.

One sailor told us he once had asked Mike why he didn't feel fear when he raced a sailboat around the world. "It's too exciting," Mike had replied.

This was a memorial service to celebrate Mike's life. We came together and shared our memories of him as well as some of his thoughts, words and loves. For a time after the services, we mingled a bit and talked.

I think most of us exited with a sailor's sense of comradship. Whatever he had gone through in his final hours, his ordeal on the North Atlantic was over. We would not see him again, but he had left us doing what he wanted to do.

Those who had been privileged to spend time with Mike had their lives enriched. We admired his quiet courage and we were astonished by his giant deeds.

With his dreams and his passion, he had achieved so much in such a short period of time we could not fully comprehend that the North Atlantic had finally claimed him. He was our hero.

It was night when I drove out of the parking lot. My headlights shone over a dark lake that lapped at the shore. The trees were bare, with their thin branches swaying in the chill north wind.

E XACTLY WHAT HAPPENED TO MIKE AND *Coyote* will never be fully known. His body was never found – and his death probably will remain a mystery of the sea.

Some sailors theorized that *Coyote* could have hit something in the water, such as a sunken container, or even a whale. But this seems improbable and the report of the Coast Guard investigation published in July, 1995, stated that there was "virtually no significant damage to the *Coyote* other than the fact that the bulb was missing."

The report went on to say that the fin showed "no signs of being crushed or struck by any object. The sides of the foil showed no signs of impact either. Finally, the hull itself was intact and undamaged. Were the *Coyote* to have struck a submerged object, the object would have had to have been at the same precise depth as *Coyote's* bulb."

Ominously, the report concluded: "It appears that the only submerged object that struck the *Coyote's* keel bulb was the muddy bottom of the Chesapeake Bay."

THE COAST GUARD REPORT FOCUSED ON the design and construction of *Coyote's* fin keel and ballast bulb. With her draft of roughly 14 feet, *Coyote's* hull drew 1 foot 3 inches of water. Her fin itself was 11 feet 2 inches deep. Below the fin's bottom hung the 18-inch-deep 8,400-pound ballast bulb.

The fin keel itself was 45 inches long. The U.S. Coast Guard's Marine Casualty report showed that the fin keel was basically in three parts: The *center main keel* assembly was 32-inches long and heavily built of Kevlar and carbon fibers. In addition, the keel had a *leading edge* of 3 inches and a *trailing edge* of 9.8 inches. The front and aft edges were of relatively soft foam and fiberglass filler construction to give the foil its shape. The exact foil length was 44.9 inches. It was about 6 inches wide.

The ballast bulb was 112-inch long and molded of lead. Originally, Mike wanted to attach a tungsten keel bulb, which would be smaller and offer less drag in the water, but the cost was prohibitive to him at $80,000. Mike had to settle for a lead bulb that cost $10,000.

Though the ballast bulb snugged up to a plate on the 45-inch long fin keel, it actually relied for its fastening strength on the center 32-inch-long main keel assembly, the Coast Guard report pointed out. It also said that this arrangement gave the 112-inch long bulb an enormous leverage upon a short span as *Coyote* pounded through heavy weather. In the racer's drive across the stormy ocean, the fin must have had tremendous forces upon it.

The foil emanated a humming noise and a vibration that Mike and other crewmembers aboard *Coyote* could hear and feel during

COYOTE'S KEEL FIN & BALLAST BULB

THREE-PART KEEL FIN
45 INCHES LONG, 6 INCHES WIDE
11 FEET, 2 INCHES DEEP

1/ MAIN (CENTER) KEEL SECTION: 32
INCHES LONG, 6 INCHES WIDE;
CONSTRUCTION: CARBON FIBER AND
KEVLAR, WITH BIRCH PLYWOOD CORE
2/ LEADING EDGE: 3 INCHES
FOAM AND FIBERGLASS FILLER
3/ TRAILING EDGE: 9.8 INCHES
FOAM AND FIBERGLASS FILLER

BULB

LOA: 112 INCHES
HEIGHT: 18 INCHES
MATERIAL: LEAD 8,400 POUNDS

FIN KEEL

THREE-PART
45 INCHES LONG

1/ MAIN (CENTER)
KEEL SECTION
32 INCHES LONG
CARBON FIBER
& KEVLAR
11 FEET 2 INCHES
DEEP

**3/ TRAILING
EDGE**
9.8 INCHES
FOAM &
FIBERGLASS
FILLER

2/ LEADING EDGE:
3 INCHES WOOD &
FIBERGLASS FILLER

FACE PLATE
INSET INTO KEEL
AND BONDED WITH
LAYERS OF
CARBON FIBER

31-INCH LONG FACE PLATE:
1/2 INCH THICK STAINLESS
STEEL

3/4 INCH DIAMETER
STAINLESS STEEL
BOLTS
THREADED &
CAPPED WITH NUTS
TO CENTER STAIN-
LESS FACE PLATE

BALLAST BULB
CAST LEAD 8,400 POUNDS
18INCHES IN DIAMETER

BALLAST BULB LENGTH 112 INCHES

ILLUSTRATION BY MARLIN BREE

*Based on specifications in Coast Guard report.
Art is not to exact scale.*

tests, the Coast Guard Report noted. It reported that a number of individuals looked at the keel's foil and bulb through the *Coyote's* sight glass while the vessel was underway, but "none of those persons, however, reported seeing any movement of the keel or bulb as the vessel worked in the seas."

The report concluded on this point that "the effect these vibrations had on the joint securing the bulb to the foil is unknown."

THE TWO GROUNDINGS IN CHESAPEAKE BAY'S MUD, however soft they may have been, drew the attention of the Coast Guard investigation: "The grounding that the *Coyote* experienced in Chesapeake Bay was probably the single largest contributing factor to the loss of the vessel's keel bulb."

It explained that efforts to free the vessel while it was stuck in the bottom "resulted in the bulb being twisted and dragged through the mud. In addition, the entire weight of the vessel shifted across the bulb while the vessel was aground. The vessel originally grounded with a 15 – 18 degrees list to starboard. The *Coyote* tacked and began to list to port, but remained stuck in the mud. As the vessel tacked the list changed from starboard to port. This caused the weight of the hull to momentary shift across and be partially supported by the keel as the vessel 'flopped' from an 18 degree list to starboard, through the vertical and then over to a list to port."

The report concluded that "the 112-inch-long lead bulb extended 34 inches forward of the foil and 45 inches aft of the foil. The twisting and dragging of the bulb, and the shifting of the vessel's weight across the keel, most likely weakened the 31-inch joint that fastened the bulb to the foil."

"At the time of the grounding," the Coast Guard report said, "none of the parties aboard felt that it was serious enough of an incident to require that the *Coyote* be hauled out of the water or to have the keel inspected. The Concordia project manager, however, did feel the incident was serious enough to conduct an internal examination of the vessel. The responsibility for deciding whether or not to dry dock the *Coyote* after the grounding was Mike Plant's. He did not have the vessel dry docked, nor did he have any divers examine the keel. Considering the fact that the keel was a new design, it would have been prudent to have the vessel inspected after the grounding."

The Coast Guard noted that "the fact that the vessel was not launched until September of 1992, due to financial delays, probably influenced Plant's decision not to dry dock the vessel. He was on a tight schedule from the day the vessel was launched through to the day he departed New York City for France. His schedule did not allow for unanticipated delays such as hauling the vessel out of the water."

THOUGH THE FIN KEEL ITSELF SURVIVED THE CAPSIZE and was recovered with *Coyote*, the ballast bulb was missing. The Coast Guard reported that *Coyote's* bulb was fastened to a stainless steel faceplace that was about ½ inch thick and had six holes cut into it and threaded. Each hole had a ¾ inch nut welded into its bottom. Stainless steel bolts came up through the ballast bulb into both the threaded faceplate and the nuts, for a minimum of 1½ inches of threaded steel.

The Coast Guard report said that an overlap laminate of 15 layers of carbon fiber helped secure *Coyote's* plate to the base of the keel. The report also said that Mike was "comfortable with the design and felt it was satisfactory."

When *Coyote* was recovered, the Coast Guard noted, "There was virtually no significant damage to the *Coyote* other than the fact that the bulb was missing."

The Coast Guard stated that that "the loss of the *Coyote's* keel bulb was a failure of the carbon fiber materials used to secure the 8,400 pound bulb assembly to the base of the keel's foil. When the material failed, the bulb assembly – which included the lead bulb, the keel bolts, and, the stainless steel plate – dropped off of the keel and the *Coyote* capsized."

TOWARD THE END, Mike probably was at the helm, sitting in the dark beside his big wheel. It was after midnight on the stormy North Atlantic and the seas were rough. Black waves big as islands roared toward him.

He probably was running on the last of his adrenalin reserves, taking pride in his big racer's handling and speed. It kept him going. He had been hand steering for days on end and he probably was having a terrible time keeping awake and concentrating

− yet he knew he could not sleep. Though he was toughing it out mentally, he was physically probably almost overwhelmed by a combination of fatigue and cold.

He was probably telling himself he and his boat could make it if they'd just hang in there. He'd hand steered for days before. Ahead lay port − he could sleep then.

His boat was ripping along, tacking hard into the wind, her sails sheeted in nearly flat, her mast and rigging taking a lot of pressure, despite being deeply reefed. Mike had reefed down to the third reef in his mainsail, putting up only 444 square foot of sail area. The big forward genoa was furled and he was tacking with his relatively tiny 250-square-foot storm jib. Perhaps he was thinking of powering down some more.

Coyote's hull was probably working hard, slamming through the oncoming waves with water rushing over the lee rail. Shock was being transmitted throughout *Coyote's* long hull. Mike heard and felt it with every jolt in his tired and bruised body.

Reconstructing the final moments, it seems apparent that Mike was pretty much on course and sticking to his intended route east to France.

B ELOW THE HULL, immense forces were at work. As the relatively flat hull pounded up and down, the 8,400-pound bulb ballast and keel fought to keep the giant racer upright. As *Coyote* crashed into the faces of oncoming waves and fought to raise her bow, there were huge twists and pressures on the end plate.

The noise and vibrations probably were worse than ever. There might have been other warnings Mike would have felt earlier, had the boat not been moving so quickly or making so much noise with her battle with the storm.

Or if he had not been so fatigued.

It was not as if he had a choice: he was nearing the middle of the stormy North Atlantic and he probably felt his safety and refuge lay dead ahead. He had to push on to the best of his ability and, like other sailors, keep the faith that his boat would hold together. He had fought against the odds before and he had won.

He had water ballast in the port ballast tank to help stabilize the boat on its low port tack, probably heading off at speed through the waves. *Coyote* did everything at speed.

Coyote's sails were loaded up when he felt a different sort of motion. The hull vibrated badly. Suddenly, the deck slammed under his feet.

From somewhere below, there was a final cracking, shattering noise.

A shuddering probably shot through the hull. The damaged carbon fiber holding the bulb plate had finally worn through and snapped, with a bang-like noise. The ballast bulb, along with the keel bolts and the stainless steel plate, dropped off the base as a single unit.

When the ballast weight was released, *Coyote's* hull bounced up a little. She probably went off course, began to slow and heel over.

Dark, green water began marching up her leeward rail.

The pressure of the wind and oncoming waves were too much. The beamy hull probably slowly reared up on its side. *Coyote* became quiet, almost eerily so.

She hung there for a minute, then went over, hard. Still on a port tack, her long boom with reefed sails caught in the water, then swung back viciously toward the boat's centerline. The boom cracked under the pressure, broke off, and was swept back. All that remained was the first two feet where it was attached to its gooseneck near the base of the mast.

As the tip of her 85-foot mast speared the water, it began to bend and finally snapped several feet above the deck. It slammed back against the cockpit, crushing the top of the cabin doghouse. The broken mast then trailed below the overturned hull, held by the stainless steel rigging, sails still hanked on. In the capsize, gear had gone flying.

Fatally wounded, *Coyote* came to rest upside down, her desperate battle to cross the North Atlantic over. All was quiet, save for the sound of the wind and the waves.

EXACTLY WHAT HAPPENED to Mike Plant that dark night on the North Atlantic remains one of the enduring mysteries of the seas. Had Mike been uninjured and able stay with his boat, or, if he had been pitched in the water and able to swim back to *Coyote* after the capsize, she would have sheltered him.

Even overturned, her bottom floated high on its five airtight chambers and there would have been more than sufficient air pockets to live under. Probably, he could have fashioned the underside of a bunk to keep him out of the water, just as other survivors of a similar capsizes had done. He had provisions and survival gear on board and the hull rode high on the water.

Not an organization given to speculation, the Coast Guard succinctly concluded its report in this manner:

"Mike Plant probably was killed when the vessel capsized."

The report added that, "Had he survived for a period of time afterwards, he would have remained with the vessel and marked the hull in some fashion to indicate he was inside – such as by putting a rag through the sight glass in the hull. He also would have tethered the EPIRB to the vessel to prevent it from drifting away and inflated the life raft to be able to get out of the water. The water temperature in the area where the vessel was located was 55 degrees F. Survival time for a person submerged in water of this temperature is less than 2 hours. Had Mr. Plant survived the vessel capsizing, it is unknown if he would have survived until 22 November 1992 or if he would have succumbed to exposure.

"Because it is unknown where or when the vessel capsizing occurred, the weather at the time of the capsizing is also unknown. The onscene weather on 26 November 1992 consisted of 25-knot winds and 5 – 7 meter seas. This weather may have been a lingering result of the storm, which passed to the north 3 weeks earlier. Whether Mike Plant was in the vicinity of the storm or if the weather additionally contributed to the casualty is unknown."

O N OCTOBER 27, the day Mike is presumed to have been lost, his EPIRB emitted three short bursts before it was forever silenced and lost. The unit was never recovered when the overturned vessel was found and inspected in the water. Like most racers, Mike had mounted his EPIRB inside the vessel's cabin on the starboard side so that a boarding wave would not knock it off the boat from its manual release or, worse, set it off. It would be handy, but he'd have to reach inside the cabin to activate it.

Why did it only emit an incomplete and misleading signal? Sailors give varying rationales on why this happened. One is that in the moments he had left, Mike sensed something was fatally wrong and in the darkness, reached for his EPIRB. He pulled it out of its holder and managed to trigger the switch. One blink, two, three – only to have the disaster cut his signals short.

The second explanation offered is that the EPIRB was knocked out of its mount during the capsize and had only a few seconds to emit a few signals before it, or its antenna, was smashed by falling rigging or the overturning hull.

Most sailors feel the only way for an EPIRB to go off is for someone to set it off.

The Coast Guard report says: "..when the vessel was recovered in January of 1993 – approximately 3 months after the capsizing – it was noted that the manual release on the mounting bracket had been opened, but the hydrostatic release had not. Whether this was opened by Plant or somehow knocked loose by debris awash in the Coyote's cabin after the capsizing is unknown. If Plant did not release the EPIRB, then it probably remained inside of the *Coyote's* cabin for some period of time until it was eventually washed out as the vessel worked in the seaway. This could explain why the device failed to operate properly."

I T WAS OVER COFFEE at the Minneapolis Boat Show that I again met up with Capt. Thom Burns and we began discussing Mike Plant and his final hours. The ex-naval officer told me he believed the scenario went something like this:

"The bulb fell off the boat and the boat went over probably to 80 or 90 degrees at first. Mike pulled the EPIRB out and whatever else he could grab as the boat was going turtle, probably in less than a minute. The EPIRB fired off a few signals before it was trapped under the boat. Mike may have been trapped there also or just been unable to get back on the overturned hull or in it. The hull composite would not sink, which kept the boat afloat in an 'awash' state. But Mike was in an exhausted state from manually steering hundreds of miles, so his probability of survival was greatly diminished from both the catastrophic event and his physical and mental state of exhaustion."

T HERE IS ANOTHER MYSTERY to unravel, that of the critical loss of power on about the third day at sea which rendered Mike's autopilots, computers, and, radios useless. The Coast Guard report analyzes this with guarded words: the "cause of the vessel's loss of power is not known, but it appears to be linked to a failure of the manual backup control for the voltage regulation system while Plant was underway."

It adds that the supplier of the equipment had recommended that a new manual control for the backup voltage regulation system be installed on *Coyote*. "The new system was not installed," the Coast Guard report says, "even though the parts were delivered to the vessel in New York prior to the beginning of Plant's voyage to France. The decision to forgo installation of the new system was probably based on the time constrains which were being felt by Mr. Plant."

A contributing factor to *Coyote's* power failure was that the engines that drove the alternators were "underpowered for the demands placed upon them. This fact necessitated the installation of the complex voltage regulation system."

IN THE DRAMA OF MAN AGAINST THE SEA, Mike was a realist. He had been through a capsize before in the Indian Ocean, in chill waters, and, he had survived.

Capsizing was not high on his priorities of dangers. Instead he felt that "the worst thing that could happen is hitting something. But I really don't think about the boat ever sinking."

He was correct: *Coyote* never sank.

EPILOGUE

O<small>N</small> J<small>ANUARY</small> 26, 1993, *C<small>OYOTE</small> WAS AGAIN FOUND*. Incredibly, she had drifted to a position about 60 miles south and west from the Irish Coast. To bring her in, the tug *Ventenor* secured towing lines to the overturned *Coyote's* foil and to both of her rudders. Ignobly, *Coyote* was towed stern first to Cobh Harbor in Cork County, Ireland. Reports say that the inside of her hull had been pretty much gutted by wave action.

A Post Casualty Inspection, as contained in the Coast Guard Report, said that *Coyote's* two forward forestays, which had self-furling foresails, appeared to be in the furled position. The back forestay, also known as the "baby stay," contained the tack of the storm jib which was, the Coast Guard reported, "all that was left of the sail."

The report stated that water ballast was found in the vessel's portside water ballast tanks. It concluded, "The fact that the storm jib was flying, that the self-furling sails were furled, and that the water ballast was in the port ballast tanks, indicates that the *Coyote* may have been sailing in heavy weather on a port tack when it capsized."

It added, "An equally likely explanation for Plant's using the storm jib is that the autopilots were not functioning due to the power failure. This would have required Plant to steer the vessel manually. Flying the storm jib would have made the *Coyote* easier to handle and less fatiguing over the duration of the voyage."

She was hauled aboard a freighter for her trans-Atlantic trip back to the U.S. There were no cheering crowds to greet her arrival back in the U.S.

Though Mike never knew it, insurance for *Coyote* had been approved while he was at sea.

News reports told of surveyors checking over her hull. Incredibly, after months adrift on the open Atlantic, she was pronounced sound after extensive ultrasound testing, but to add additional stiffness, designer Rodger Martin added an interior skeleton of carbon fiber tubing. She got a lighter, more streamlined deckhouse, a bowsprit, and a reconfigured rig to carry more sail area as well as a new keel and bulb. In the rebuild, she got even faster after shedding about 1,000 pounds of weight.

On Aug 28, 1994, she was returning from her first major voyage after being rebuilt when she collided with a fishing boat.

Coyote's strong hull was reportedly undamaged, but the 62-foot fishing boat began taking on water. Coast Guard planes dropped pumps to crewmembers to keep flooding under control.

Undaunted, she returned to racing. With David Scully as her skipper, *Coyote* finally got her around-the-world run. She successfully circled the globe in the BOC 1994-95 race and came in fourth. With an admirable total time of 133 days 56 minutes and 35 seconds, she averaged 8.21 knots.

She placed second in her class in the 1996 Europe One Star Transatlantic Race.

Mike's family established the Mike Plant Fund at the Minnetonka Yacht Club to help underprivileged children participate in sailing programs. Each year, kids from throughout the area learn to sail in the same waters that Mike sailed on as a boy.

On September 6, 2002, in a ceremony held in Newport, Mike Plant was inducted into the Museum of Yachting's Single Handed Sailor's Hall of Fame.

His friend, Herb McCormick, said at the dedication ceremonies:

"One of the great tragedies of Mike's passing is the awful timing. Here he was, finally, after three circumnavigations, truly ready to contend for the crown. If all went well, if he had that mix of luck and execution required of all champions, he was ready to challenge the best on his own terms. He was ready to live his biggest dream."

For more information and commentary,
please refer to the Author's Notes.

THE DAY
ALL HELL
BROKE
LOOSE

Aboard Persistence at Grand Portage: the author waits for swirling fog banks to lift off Superior

PROLOGUE

THE WAITING WAS THE HARDEST. For four days, I had been tied up to a weather-beaten dock, eager to begin my voyage. Off to the north was pine-covered Mt. Josephine and at water's edge, the pointed-tip wooden stockade of the old fur fort. This was rugged, historic Grand Portage, MN, at one time the edge of civilization for the Eastern world.

My boat, *Persistence*, was in the "pocket," protected behind a large, broken breakwall and in front of a rusty barge, partly sunk on its side. Not far away lay the Witch's Tree, and beyond lay Lake Superior's chill waters, which surged with high winds and swirling fog banks.

When the weather cleared, I'd be off on a solo voyage into the furthest north and most remote reaches of Lake Superior, the world's

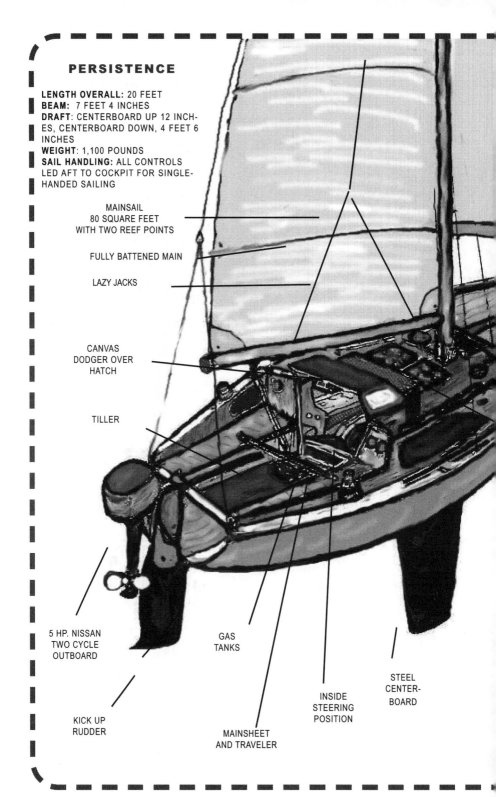

PERSISTENCE

LENGTH OVERALL: 20 FEET
BEAM: 7 FEET 4 INCHES
DRAFT: CENTERBOARD UP 12 INCH-
ES, CENTERBOARD DOWN, 4 FEET 6
INCHES
WEIGHT: 1,100 POUNDS
SAIL HANDLING: ALL CONTROLS
LED AFT TO COCKPIT FOR SINGLE-
HANDED SAILING

MAINSAIL
80 SQUARE FEET
WITH TWO REEF POINTS

FULLY BATTENED MAIN

LAZY JACKS

CANVAS
DODGER OVER
HATCH

TILLER

5 HP. NISSAN
TWO CYCLE
OUTBOARD

GAS
TANKS

STEEL
CENTER-
BOARD

INSIDE
STEERING
POSITION

KICK UP
RUDDER

MAINSHEET
AND TRAVELER

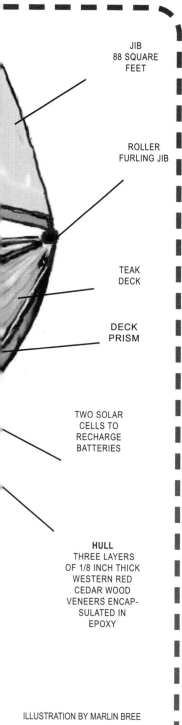

JIB
88 SQUARE
FEET

ROLLER
FURLING JIB

TEAK
DECK

DECK
PRISM

TWO SOLAR
CELLS TO
RECHARGE
BATTERIES

HULL
THREE LAYERS
OF 1/8 INCH THICK
WESTERN RED
CEDAR WOOD
VENEERS ENCAP-
SULATED IN
EPOXY

ILLUSTRATION BY MARLIN BREE

largest freshwater lake. Ahead lay an archipelago of islands that were some of boating's best-kept secrets: a land of mists, fog and very uncertain weather.

This was wilderness country, where you could sail for days without seeing another boat or person. Legend had it that some people went into these islands each year and never returned. Probably that was true at one time, but I was equipped with modern radios and GPS. I'd be OK.

I felt it was high time to make my voyage. The Canadian Government had plans to make this the world's largest freshwater marine conservation area: roughly 11,000 square kilometers that stretches from the Sleeping Giant Mountain to the Slate Islands. It's a big area that comprises nearly one seventh of the giant lake's total surface.

I wanted to sail the Northern Arc while it was still wild and free.

Impatiently, I listened to the wind moan. The unsettled weather couldn't last long.

Then I'd be off.

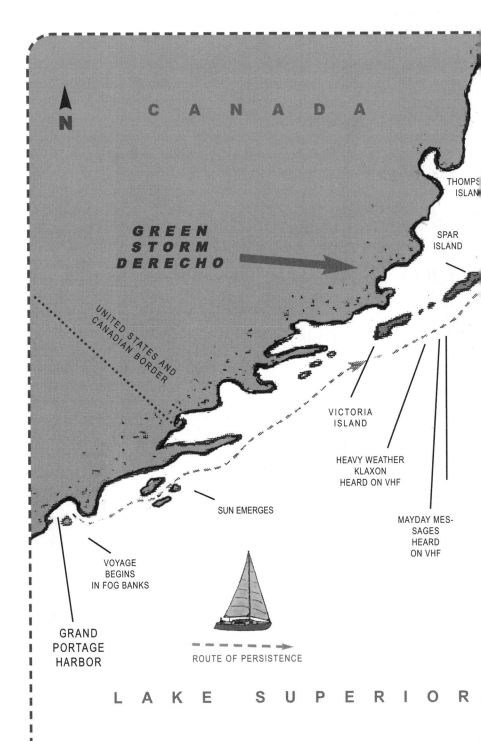

N

C A N A D A

GREEN
STORM
DERECHO

THOMPS
ISLAN

SPAR
ISLAND

UNITED STATES AND
CANADIAN BORDER

VICTORIA
ISLAND

HEAVY WEATHER
KLAXON
HEARD ON VHF

SUN EMERGES

MAYDAY MES-
SAGES
HEARD
ON VHF

VOYAGE
BEGINS
IN FOG BANKS

GRAND
PORTAGE
HARBOR

ROUTE OF PERSISTENCE

L A K E   S U P E R I O R

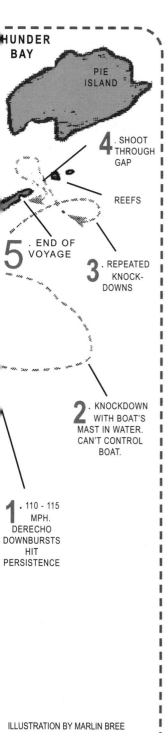

HUNDER
BAY

PIE
ISLAND

4. SHOOT
THROUGH
GAP

REEFS

5. END OF
VOYAGE

3. REPEATED
KNOCK-
DOWNS

2. KNOCKDOWN
WITH BOAT'S
MAST IN WATER.
CAN'T CONTROL
BOAT.

1. 110 - 115
MPH.
DERECHO
DOWNBURSTS
HIT
PERSISTENCE

ILLUSTRATION BY MARLIN BREE

THE DAY ALL HELL BROKE LOOSE

A small boat
meets the
Storm of the Century

A COLD MASS OF THICK, GRAY FOG hung ominously across the Sawtooth Mountains, but here in the small fjord-like bay, the waters were clear blue down to their icy depths.

I was at the helm of my 20-foot sailboat, *Persistence*, on the start of my solo adventure on Lake Superior. My 5 h.p. Nissan outboard was running easily at about a third throttle and I felt reasonably confident. Early on, I had switched my VHF radio to NOAA weather radio, which had assured me that it would be the hottest day of the year with a possibilities of thunderstorms later in the day.

So far, so good. I tapped my onboard barometer and the needle rose just a twitch to indicate fair weather.

On Grand Portage Bay, the small island was wrapped in the cotton-candy gray stuff and the north of the bay, where a historic 18th-century fort should be showing its spiked wooden stockades, also was wreathed in fog. In the marina office, I struck up a conversation with a local veteran boater. "Oh, the fog'll burn off," he said. "I'd go."

So I shoved off, seemingly aloft on the

transparent, glacial inland sea, ducking in and out of the spectral fog and running down my pre-set global positioning system way-points.

In the fluky, light air, I was motoring with my sails uncovered, ready to hoist. Entering the chilly fog banks was like entering a tomb: cold and damp, despite my layers of wool socks, thermal underwear and polar fleece.

It was hard to believe that today was the Fourth of July.

Though I expected an easy run across the Canadian border to an island guarding the mouth of Thunder Bay, I had prepared my boat for the open waters of Superior. The forward hatch was dogged tightly closed and my boat's weight was centered. (I had taken my sleeping bag, duffel bags of gear, food, provisions, and anything else I could get out of the ends, and lashed them along-side the centerboard trunk.) I had carefully had gone over the boat to be certain there were no loose lines and the rigging was taut. I buckled into my safety harness and laid out my GPS, nau-tical chart and an area cruising guide.

My VHF was tuned to channel 16. I was in range of Grand Portage and its marina, but as soon as I crossed the border, I'd be in range of the Canadian Coast Guard station at Thunder Bay, Ontario.

WHEN I EMERGED from the fog bank, my heavy weather pre-cautions seemed unnecessary. The sun was high and bright. Below me, clear waters sparkled down to their glacier-carved blue depths, and off to port, beautiful little islands lifted out of the waterline, green with small fir trees. I began to enjoy myself.

As soon as I crossed the border, I began to rue my layers of fleece and thermal gear. Perspiration lined my brow and my glasses wore a little haze from overheating.

Lifting my long-billed baseball cap, I brushed my brow with the back of my gloved hand and looked up at the shoreline's high crests. That layer of fog still hadn't burned off. In fact, it looked denser, heavier and slightly sinister.

My VHF radio was crackly, but its speaker blared an unmis-takable klaxon. It was Thunder Bay's Coast Guard giving me a storm warning.

I looked around: I was on the open water with an inhospitable shoreline to port and many reefs in between. Ahead lay a small island with a tiny cove – only 20 minutes away.

I cranked up the engine to three-quarter power. Over the Nissan's racket, I heard the dread words, *"Mayday, Mayday!"* Somewhere a sailboat had overturned and three people struggled in the water.

O UT OF NOWHERE, a monster jumped over the mountains and began to swing my mast from side to side. I heard the sound of a wall of wind passing through the shrouds, beginning with a low moan and then moving from a howl to a shriek. My boat bucked out of control, slewing to one side, as I frantically tried to get the bow downwind – the classic heavy weather storm tactic.

But the wind had the boat in its grip, shoving *Persistence* faster and faster. Suddenly, I flew forward as my boat nosed into the waves, bow down, stern up in a semi-pitch pole.

A sharp, stabbing pain hit my right side as I slammed into the cabin headfirst. Above me, a port light turned a bright green – the entire side of the boat was underwater. I saw water splash up through the centerboard trunk.

My boat seemed to teeter for a small eternity, balancing on its side and nearly turning over. There was a sudden lurch and I had an instant vision of myself in the dark, trapped below, churning furiously in heart-stopping cold waters and having to swim down to get out. I thought of clambering atop my overturned hull to hang on for as long as I could while the storm carried me out into the middle of the lake.

Wham. A duffel of foul weather clothing followed by bags of groceries and a plastic carton fell on me.

The wind screamed like a banshee. Behind me, my engine howled – its prop out of the water.

The boat lurched again.

S UDDENLY, I was lying on my back, looking up. I saw my alarm clock and other gear fly from one side of my boat to the other.

It took me several bewildered seconds before I realized what had happened. The winds had caught my boat and thrown it forward. It went faster and faster and stopped abruptly. with the stern flying up and the bow digging in. I'd been dumped forward into the cabin. I lay dazed in the starboard quarter berth with my feet over my head.

My mind sent out little queries: Was I in much pain? Did I break anything. What was I going to do if *Persistence* capsized all the way, mast down, bottom up? I braced myself.

There was another little lurch. *Time to move.* Somehow, I pulled myself up and tore out into the cockpit. Rain like lead drops pelted my face as I faced my enemy.

The lake was cold and gray, its face blasted flat by the terrible wind. Long contrails of mist whipped across the water like icy whips. Four heavy rubber fenders that had been lying in the cockpit simply bounced up and flew away.

My boat teetered on its side, reeling with every gust. The starboard mast spreader dipped into the water, rose a little unsteadily, and then hung in mid-air.

I held onto the portside lifeline, still in my safety harness. Hand over hand, I worked my way back to the transom. My hand closed in a death grip on the tiller.

A NOTHER HUGE GUST TORE INTO THE BOAT. I felt it go further down.

I threw myself over the windward lifelines as far as I could, but the boat was on its side and out of control. I could only hang on. My weight seemed to make no difference.

Then, after what seemed like an eternity, the mast soared upright and the hull came down with a mighty splash.

The engine's out-of-control racing stopped as the prop bit solid water. I could feel the rudder go back into the water.

I held my breath. Nothing broken.

The boat picked up speed.

I jammed the tiller over. *Persistence* headed directly downwind, taking the wild gusts on the transom instead of the vulnerable beam. That didn't seem to help all that much. In the wind's gusts, the mast seemed to want to squirrel down into the water.

The wind slammed into *Persistence* again. Down went the mast, up came the water, and out I went, leaning over the edge. It occurred again and again in a maddening battle of knockdowns.

I was shivering uncontrollably, soaked clear through. I couldn't see very well, since my glasses were misted over with water.

I was in a world of hurt. I had to no place to run, no place to hide and nobody to help me.

A NOTHER VIOLENT GUST hit the boat. I heard a "ping." Something had snapped.

I saw the furled mainsail come loose from its shock cords. The wind's icy fingers began to shove it up the mast. The big sail reared a third of the way up, flapping, rattling and catching the wind.

My heart pounded. The boat was already on the edge of capsizing all the way. What would happen with the sail up?

I could not leave the helm. The only answer was to run on with the wind until something else broke or the storm let up.

I clenched my teeth and tightened my grip on the tiller.

I RAN ON INTO THE RAGING LAKE until I sensed the wind letting up a little; at least the insane gusts were not shoving the boat down so far.

"Do it!" I steeled myself. Timing the gusts, I shoved the tiller over hard – and hung on. *Persistence* did a dangerous dip to leeward, hung down on its rail for a moment, and the dark waters rushed up.

I had the boat and faced the wind. The sail rattled and whipped on the mast; the boat felt terribly unstable underneath me.

I needed more power in the teeth of the storm. One hand on the tiller, I reached back and gave the engine full throttle and locked it there.

The 5-horsepower Nissan outboard bellowed and dug in. The boat bounced up and down, careening sideways on the waves. Sometimes the prop was in the water; sometimes out. The little Nissan revved unmercifully and screamed.

Through my rain-splashed eyeglasses, I could make out an island ahead. *How could this be?*

I had already passed Spar Island and had been abeam of the rock shoals leading to Thompson Island.

I glanced at my water-soaked chart.

I had been blown off course, circled around, and was now heading back to barren, rocky Spar Island.

A s I FOUGHT MY WAY NEARER TO THE ISLAND, I could only hope that it was bold and deep to its shoreline. I'd have to take a chance on the reefs. To starboard lay some rocky pinnacles, their dark teeth awash with white foam.

As I came into its lee, the island deflected some of the main blasts. I throttled back, judging my rate of speed with the wind's grip on my mast and boat. My heart was pounding and my muscles were knotted tight. I was shivering uncontrollably and I was gasping in the cold rain. I hurt.

Shakily, I wiped my glasses with my fingers. Ahead lay a row of spectacular rocky spars, slashed with waves and spray. They stretched from the northeastern edge of Spar Island out into the lake.

In the distance, through the rain, I could make out a gray headland. It had to be Thompson Island.

I twisted the throttle, and the boat roared ahead and again caught the brunt of the storm. *Persistence* staggered, her speed diminished, her rail dipping low into the water. Wind shrieked in the rigging, wrestling with the mast. I edged out over the port side, my leg locked around the traveler beam, one arm around a winch. Small, rocky islets – spray everywhere – flew by.

I was desperate to reach Thompson Cove. I reached down for my chart and a cruising guidebook, which I had jammed to one side of my gas tank. Both were soaked; ink was running where I had marked my course. I dared not let the wind get these – my only guides to the Lake Superior wilderness ahead.

I wished I could move forward to grab my GPS unit, programmed for the coordinates to Thompson cove. But I dared not leave my steering. I'd just have to wait until I found the harbor.

I reasoned with myself through rain-clouded glasses. I was headed for a small cove on a small island. How tough could that be? I'd just run alongside Thompson Island, far enough out to avoid any reefs, but close enough to see the cove.

I checked my watch. I had told the Thunder Bay Coast Guard that I'd be in that harbor in 45 minutes. All I had to do was maintain course and eyeball the cove.

I had time to spare.

A S I CAME UNDER THE LEE OF THOMPSON, the island shouldered the wind off me. I breathed a sigh of relief and scanned the shoreline. I slipped past a large cove, but there was no entrance. I was rapidly approaching the end of the island. If I ran alongside to the island's tip, I'd have to come across the entry to the cove. Easy.

I glanced at my NOAA chart again to look at the tiny island. There was nothing officially designated as Thompson Cove. The name only appeared in my cruising guidebook. In the jouncing, rain-soaked cockpit, that was hard to read.

Scanning the shore, I saw a rocky cliff leading down to the water's edge, its crest topped with trees. Farther away, lashed by waves and spray, a small, round island stood its lonely sentinel.

Off in the distance, I saw a dark blue line etched on the water. It was moving – rushing toward me.

That much blue on the water meant only one thing: wind. Tons of it.

Howling, the storm had switched from the west, veering to catch me again.

The first blasts shook my boat. The tiller twisted in my hand as my boat bucked and took a dive to starboard. The boat was over down on her side, with the cabin going partly under and mast spreaders dipping in the water. Icy waves climbed the side of my boat, splashing into the cockpit.

Where was the cove?

I neared a dangerous place — a gap between the land and a small island. A wave tore at the rocks, flinging spray high into the air. As the boat raced on, I shuddered: a teeth of reefs lay just under the waves.

Beyond lay something green. I took a deep breath. Adrenaline surging, I charged the gap with the engine cranked up to full.

Suddenly, I lost control. In a heart-stopping moment, the boat careened dangerously toward the islet's foam-lashed reefs.I swore, prayed, steered and shifted my weight around.

Finally, the boat came back up and obeyed me.

I circled to try again.

This time, I went further east, letting the tiny islet take the blast of the waves and wind. I braced myself, squeezing the throttle hard to be certain I had every last ounce of power the engine could give me. I charged – bouncing, careening and splashing.

I made it through the gap.

Then, I was facing huge, square rollers – the worst waves I'd fought all day.

M Y SPEEDING BOW SPEARED into the first oncoming tower; the impact shook the boat. The bow disappeared, but the water kept coming over the cabin top and hit me in the chest. I groaned at the chill.

I climbed the wave, teetering at the top. For the first time, I could see what lay ahead. Something was terribly wrong.

It finally came to me: That big, distinctive island that lay ahead was none other than Pie Island. I had overshot my destination.

I could not live out here.

D ESPERATELY, I TIMED THE WAVES and on the back of one of the steep chargers, I turned the boat around. I was flying now, surfing the waves, almost out of control.

Ahead, the gap loomed, but I made it through.

I was growing very tired: my reactions were slowing, and it was hard to think. I was doused in icy water, cold to my core.

I roared at full throttle back up Thompson Island, looking for the lost cove. Rocky slopes rushed close by my speeding boat. Beyond one crag, I saw something shining up high, above the trees.

Unmistakably, they were the tips of sailboat masts.

As I cut in, the water widened. On one side was a high outcrop of rock, and on the other, a spruce-covered hill. In between, still, blue water.

It was blessed, beautiful Thompson Cove.

C ANADIAN BOATERS were helping me tie up when I heard my VHF: "Calling the sailboat *Persistence*."

It was the Thunder Bay Coast Guard. I was overdue on my ETA and they were ready to initiate a search-and-rescue mission. I had not heard them when I was in the cockpit, surrounded by the noise of the storm, flapping sail and engine.

"Sorry," I apologized. "But I've been little busy."

Photo / Clive Dudley

EPILOGUE

THAT NIGHT, waves raged against the island's rocky crags and I had difficulty falling asleep. Sometime between 1 or 2 a.m., I awakened to rain pelting hard on the wooden cabin top. I peered into the blackness of the harbor, more than a little worried. Though I had managed to put a nylon tarp over my open cockpit, I had my wet clothing from the storm out there to dry out.

I dashed out to haul them back inside the cabin, but they were soaked. Dumping the soggy mess on the floorboards, I crawled back into my bunk, chilled to the bone. I was having a hard time warming up, even with long johns, wool socks, fleece, and lying in two sleeping bags covered with a fleece blanket.

"This is July," I reminded myself, between shivers.Once again, I thought of turning back, hauling my boat out of the water and going home.

The next day dawned clear and bright, with glorious sunshine drying out my soggy boat. I was in a great mood as I stepped into the cockpit and, out of curiosity, grabbed one of the stainless steel shrouds holding up the mast. Odd, but I didn't recall the rigging was this loose before. Then I remembered the winds that had twisted my boat around and thrown it down into the water on its beam ends. No wonder the rigging was loose – it had stretched under the pressure. I had been lucky: none of the fittings had broken. My boat had held together.

I decided I had been through the worse that Superior could throw at me and I had survived. Good fortune had to lie ahead as well as better weather. I'd continue my voyage.

It was only after I returned home that I learned I had survived the Storm of the Century – with wind downbursts and microbursts up to 115 mph. One later estimate was 130 mph. winds.

The storm was a rare progressive derecho with hurricane-force winds whose downburst clusters had torn up chunks of old-pine hilltops and scooped out deeply wooded valleys, before its blasts came out to me on Superior.

It was an infamous, dangerous storm. Somehow, my small boat and I had survived.

For more information on the voyage and about the July 4, 1999, derecho, please turn to Author's Notes

AUTHOR'S NOTES

1/ Ten Feet Across the Pacific

YANKEE GIRL'S VOYAGE from Long Beach, California, to Honolulu, Hawaii, was remarkable. Gerry Spiess took only 34 days to sail 2,200 nautical miles (2,539 statute) to Hawaii and averaged 65 nautical miles (NM) a day (74.75 statute), under all conditions, including calms. This was an extraordinary performance for a heavily laden boat with a 9-foot 9-inch waterline, especially since many larger blue water sailing craft on the same route often average 100 miles per day. Especially noteworthy was that Gerry sailed alone and was not part of a fully crewed boat. "I was asleep a third of the time," he said.

But *Yankee Girl* kept sailing faster. In the South Pacific's trade winds, *Yankee Girl* often would reel off 100 NM a day. Best day ever was 120 NM in a 24-hour run, which occurred during the last part of her trans-Pacific crossing – when Gerry said he finally learned how to sail her at her best.

"*Yankee Girl* was the last of the record-setting small boats that could actually sail and point," an admiring sailor told me. "The rest are basically downwind rafts."

Gerry not only had built the boat, but designed her. He told me he considered the six-year design challenge to be the most interesting part of the entire project. A former school teacher in White Bear, MN, he became fascinated with micro-boat voyages and the intellectual challenge to create, design and build the smallest boat that could safely cross any ocean, unaided and entirely on her own. He accomplished breakthroughs in design, construction, and small boat operations. He was brilliant, tough, resourceful and determined. As a result, there never was another boat quite like *Yankee Girl*.

Designed to carry everything needed for herself and her sailor, including huge amounts of gear and provisions, *Yankee Girl* was a monumental boat on a 9-foot 9-inch waterline. As a bare hull, she weighted less than 440 pounds. With her running gear, she weighed 750 pounds and loaded up with food and supplies practically filling her cabin, she weighed a whopping 2,200 pounds. Fully loaded for the voyage, Gerry joked, "I had to eat my way in."

Despite her size, the 10-footer had remarkable sea keeping and sailing abilities. She moved smartly on a broad reach, but most importantly, she pointed relatively high, with steadiness and speed. Most cruising sailboats can only climb upwind at about 45 degrees to the wind (90 degrees both sides combined), not the 29 degrees or so sometimes claimed. *Yankee Girl* could also point about 45 degrees, remarkable for such a small cruiser.

One of the keys to her sailing abilities was the design of her full keel. Gerry had experimented with keels and came to feel that his tiny boat needed a long keel, but not a deep one. It was a matter of balance, he felt, for if *Yankee Girl's* keel were deep, like a fin keel, the small boat would be in danger of being overpowered by a large wave and trip over its own keel. *Yankee Girl's* keel was graduated, but not deep. Amidships, for example, it was only 3 inches in depth, which provided enough lateral resistance to make the boat point, but not vulnerable to cross-waves. *Yankee Girl* would work with the ocean, not against it.

The design sometimes succeeded better than Gerry expected. When he tested the little boat in storm conditions on White Bear Lake, he found that she refused to lie to a variety of sea anchors. *Yankee Girl* would heel to one side, sail past the sea anchor and begin towing it.

Yankee Girl was strongly built for the ocean. Though most traditional wooden boats are a collection of pieces fastened together, *Yankee Girl* had her keel, stem, transom knee, deck knee and mast step laminated in a single piece. Gerry built up the keel by gluing and screwing six laminations of ¾ inch plywood for a keel 4 ½ inches thick – a virtual battering ram. Once the 3/8-inch plywood planking was glued and screwed on the frames and stringers, Gerry fiberglassed the exterior with heavy 10-ounce fiberglass cloth and polyester resin, enormously adding to the hull's strength. He likened it to a tough little "walnut."

Could the boat capsize? "No way," Gerry answered. If hit by a wave or blast of wind, she'd heel but bob right back up because the underwater compartments fully loaded weighed 2,200 pounds out of the boat's weight of 740 pounds. Initially, Gerry planned to add lead bars below, but he finally decided not to take that extra weight along. He figured he had enough ballast.

In addition to being self-righting, *Yankee Girl* was designed with positive floatation (she wouldn't sink), self-steering (she could steer herself over long stretches of ocean) and self-rescuing (the boat herself became the life raft).

Her rudder was designed to be deeper than the boat. The rudder's lower part was angled forward with a bulb, so that *Yankee Girl* had a balanced helm. Gerry began his design with an ordinary rudder, but found in sea trials that the little boat had a terrible helm in strong winds and required too much muscle. To solve the problem, he extended the rudder below and added a balance point forward. This not only civilized the tiller pressure, but added to her pointing ability.

Yankee Girl was designed to be an all-weather slugger, not just a fair-wind sailor. Based on his voyaging experience, Gerry's felt that an ocean-going voyager needs protection from the elements. ("You don't go out there to rough it; you go out there to smooth it.") *Yankee Girl* doesn't have an open cockpit like most sailboats. Instead, her cabin opens up with a large hatch cover so that, in effect, the after part of the cabin can become the open cockpit. When it is closed, the skipper can be sheltered and protected and also can steer from *inside* the closed cabin.

Despite the cabin's small dimensions, Gerry could stretch out fully in his bunk, which ran all the way along the starboard side. When I was aboard *Yankee Girl*, I found that she was surprisingly spacious and almost commodious. Somehow, she seemed larger than she was and she made me feel comfortable.

Long before he took her to sea, Gerry spent a lot of time aboard his boat, sleeping, eating and sailing. This was consistent with his philosophy never to go to sea in a new boat, only an "old boat." By that he meant a well-tried and thoroughly tested boat.

Obsessed with details, Gerry felt he had to master them all. To him, a boat was like a chain and all links had to be equally strong.

The voyage he was undertaking, as he said in *Alone Against the Atlantic*, wasn't "...a series of chance events, a time when I'd be cast adrift in a universe of incalculable dimensions. Instead, I surrounded myself with details – all of which could be isolated, analyzed and acted upon. I meant to be in control at all times."

I once asked him how he tested a Minnesota boat for an ocean passage and he told me he waited until really bad weather roared onto White Bear Lake. Deliberately sailing into the teeth of the storm, Gerry kept *Yankee Girl's* sails up during the initial blasts of the storm until she heeled unmercifully. As part of his self-imposed test, he clambered out from the protection of his enclosed cockpit to the top of the boat. His philosophy as that if he couldn't accomplish a sail change in a little Minnesota lake, he couldn't do it on the open ocean.

But in the screaming winds, *Yankee Girl's* lack of buoyancy at the bow plunged him in waters up to his knees. He got the sails down, but learned not to go all the way forward. Instead, he adapted a sort of crouch while wedged in between chain plates and mast and leaned forward to put up or take down the jib. The distance was only a couple of feet – but this worked.

On the Pacific, *Yankee Girl* packed 54 gallons of pre-mixed gas with oil, secured in plastic gas cans in the bilge. He planned to keep moving even in the doldrums by running his two-cycle engine at a fast idle. This engine speed was a compromise to keep *Yankee Girl* moving but minimized carboning and kept the engine relatively clean. On flat water with no headwind, this would result in a speed of about 2.2 knots – 2.53 statute mph.

Gerry could run his little outboard day and night for days on end. Under engine, *Yankee Girl* easily covered 50 NM per day and when he hit the Pacific current, which gave him a boost of a fraction of a knot, his total day's run under power easily could hit 60 NM. This may not seem like blazing cruising, but it was good progress for a 10-footer. Actually, his speed exceeded what the *Mayflower* did on an average day's run: the Pilgrims' 100-foot ship averaged only about 2 NM per hour and usually sailed only 48 NM per day.

Gerry liked to joke with dockside power boaters about *Yankee Girl's* cruising range under power. With their hundreds and sometimes thousands of horsepower, they often were not impressed with Gerry's little fishing engine hung out back, little suspecting the truth. "How much range do you have?" Gerry'd bait them, and the power boaters typically would reply that they had maybe a 200- to 300-mile range. Gerry would smile and tell them that *Yankee Girl* had nearly *a thousand mile range*. He did the math for them: *Yankee Girl* carried 54 gallons of pre-mix and could power 17 statute miles to a gallon. That would give him a whopping range of about *918 miles*. Of course, his 4.5-hp. outboard could push the boat faster than her usual fast-idle cruising speed of 2 ½ miles per hour, but speed was not part of his plan. He did not want to go fast, only far.

The outboard hung unprotected on a transom bracket and was exposed to every wave that came along. Sometimes during storms, the engine was hit so hard that Gerry feared it would be ripped off. More than once, Gerry looked back "just to see if it was still there." Dunked in seawater and punished by waves, it started up and ran reliably. That was after Gerry had discovered an initial fluke grounding of a kill switch and fixed the problem by bypassing the circuitry. After that, he stopped the engine by choking it off.

For clothing, he carried 35 pairs of shorts and T shirts, 35 pairs of socks, 10 pairs of pants, 28 long-sleeved shirts, in addition to a down jacket, 5 sweaters, and 2 suits of foul weather gear, plus rubber gloves (3 pairs), wool gloves (1 pair) and 5 caps. He had learned through experimentation how much clothing he could get into a plastic jug if he wrapped the items very tightly. Because he had no way to wash the salt from his garments, much less dry them, he'd wear each item only once and throw it overboard to be dissolved in the sea.

He also carried underwater epoxy, extra wood and plywood so he could repair his craft if she ever were damaged. He also had a complete tool kit aboard to do just that.

Despite his careful planning, Gerry once nearly ran out of gas. Though he had several gallons of gas left below, he had not refilled his main tank when he left his overnight Molokai anchorage because he figured he had enough gas to maneuver. But he had to motor out of his anchorage and nearing Oahu, had to run his engine to get past the lee of Diamond Head. When he entered the channel, he turned off his engine and had a windy sleigh ride into Honolulu. But nearing the Ali Wai small boat harbor, he had to fire up his outboard to maneuver because he was surrounded by well-wishers in boats. When he finally tied up in the guest of honor space in front of the yacht club, he was running on fumes. It would have been embarrassing for him to run out of gas – and have to be towed the final few yards to his destination.

After the completion of his record-setting voyage to Sydney, Australia, Gerry returned to his native Minnesota and donated *Yankee Girl* to the Minnesota Historical Society, where she became a part of the society's historical treasures. Gerry visited her from time to time when she was on public display and he told me he sometimes wished he had "his little girl" back. She is a special boat, he said, and still capable of carrying him on other ocean voyages. Though he has designed, built and owned a variety of other boats, none remains so affectionately in his heart as his "little girl" – *Yankee Girl*. He misses her.

2/ The Old Man and the Inland Sea

THE OLD-TIME NORTH SHORE FISHERMEN were amazing boaters who routinely ventured out on Superior's often treacherous waters during all weather, wave and storm conditions in small, open fishing boats.

In the early days, the boats were rowed by hand but in Helmer Aakvik's time, they were powered by small outboard engines. If an engine failed, a fisherman could still to row home and that's what Helmer counted on after his two engines failed during the ice storm.

Rowing on the Big Lake can be a sporty proposition, or so I found. One day, I took a 17-foot rowboat out on the open waters of Superior near Port Wing, WI, on the southwestern shore of Superior. The boat handled well in the calm waters of the harbor, but past the breakwaters, I knew that I had entered big water. In light waves of a foot to a foot-and-a-half, the little boat did a lively dance and bobbed along on the crests. With its Sitka Spruce oars, it glided easily, but as I worked the boat in the waves, I had to be careful of how I centered my weight. I could not imagine standing up in the small craft, much less dragging heavy fishing nets up one side. Nor would I want to be alone in such a craft to face one of Superior's late season storms. As I remembered my own rowing adventure, I felt a sense of awe for the North Shore fishermen's boating skills, determination and quiet every-day courage.

*   *   *

Carl Hammer's skiff vanished when he disappeared on Superior. Helmer Aakvik's ice-covered skiff went under the waves after he was rescued by a Coast Guard Cutter and they attempted to tow the boat. Sadly, because both skiffs were lost, I encountered differing reports on the size and design of Hammer and Aakvik's boats. News accounts reported the Hovland fishermen's boats were nearly identical 16-foot-long, flat-bottomed skiffs.

In the course of my research, Irene Malner, who grew up in Hovland, MN., was most helpful. She told me that her brother, David Hammer, had a skiff in a boat shed near the waters of Chicago Bay. It was "Dad's Old Boat," the second of Chris Hammer's identical skiffs − the one that did not go out that fateful day when brother Carl was lost. She added that Helmer's boat was similar but had slightly less freeboard and was in worse shape. Not surprisingly, it was also much older.

With her husband, Irene measured the old skiff and confirmed that it is 17 feet LOA and has a 5-foot beam. It was built with pine planking 1-inch wide by 1½-inches deep. Irene told me that the bottom had a slight angle and sent me several photographs. I enlarged the photographs in my computer and printed them. With a compass, I measured a 5- to 7-degree angle to the chine bottom − not flat at all. When I asked Irene how heavy the boat was, she said, "very."

This boat differs greatly from the skiff I was in. My boat was light and designed for rowing. The North Shore Skiff was heavy and designed to handle a small outboard on the stern. My skiff had a gently rounded bottom; the angular North Shore Skiff had a v-shaped chine hull. The chines allowed a fisherman to lean over the side and pull in a net without tipping over the boat. The North Shore boat not only had to slug it out on the open waters of Superior during inevitable storms, but also had to be tough enough to be winched up a pole slide with a full load of fish.

It seemed to me that the North Shore skiff was a splendid adaptation of design and construction by the immigrant fishermen.

*   *   *

Helmer Aakvik had emigrated from the island of Donna in Norway and lived since 1921 with his wife, Christine, in their rustic cabin overlooking Superior. The cabin had electricity as its only modern convenience. Their water supply was a bucket and the lake.

He had worked as a fisherman in the Fjords as well as in Alaskan waters and was an experienced, tough man with a fisherman's heritage of hard work and strong determination

Part of that heritage had been passed on to Carl Hammer. The grandson of a Norwegian immigrant family, Carl had grown up on the Hovland waterfront and as a youngster worked in his family's fish house, cleaning herring when his dad brought in a skiff full. In winters, Carl would help his family cut ice on Superior to store in the icehouse to ice down fish they caught in the summer.

Carl had grown to nearly 6 feet in height, with a muscular, sturdy frame. He had dark hair, and, according to his sister, "gentle brown eyes." He left Hovland to become a sailor on a U.S. Navy destroyer and later he worked as a wheelsman on ore boats that plied the Great Lakes. By the time he returned to his native Hovland, he had seen a lot of water, a lot of boats and had done a lot of boating.

Though Aakvik called him "the Kid," Carl was 26 years old and he and his wife, Ida, were expecting their first child. Thoughts of the family's expenses might have been on his mind when he went out that fateful day, just before the holiday, as the deadly storm was rising.

*   *   *

Earlier, as I voyaged along the North Shore in my 20-foot wooden sailboat, *Persistence*, I heard warnings to beware a storm called the northeaster. But in this community, it is the *northwester* that causes the greatest loss of boats and the most fishermen's deaths. Helmer and Carl had been caught in a northwester's offshore winds that roared down from Canada over the Sawtooth Mountains and blasted onto the lake to build waves and blow a boat away from shore. Fishermen have to fight their way back through increasingly big waves and broken seas.

Looking down the cliffs near Hovland, I wondered how the fishermen managed to beach their boats during storms on such a rocky shore? Large waves would be rolling off the lake, dashing against the rocks, making it difficult to land a boat in the surf. One story I heard from Irene was about her father's attempt to land a small boat among the breakers. He'd time the waves and on the seventh wave, power at high speed for the shore and run the boat's bow part way up on the slide. He'd leap from the boat onto the slide, climb the poles to the boathouse, and winch up the boat.

The procedure would be more difficult if the poles were icy, and, in the North Country, that could be anytime after October. Probably, the Old Man was concerned about landing his boat in these difficult conditions – if and when he got back.

* * *

For his research and calculations to determine the drift rate of small boats in storms on Lake Superior, I am indebted to Bosuns Mate 5th Class Paul Lentini, of the Coast Guard, Duluth. I wanted to know how far the Old Man and The Kid could have drifted during the storm. Using the Coast Guard's formula: 0.07 x wind speed in knots x 0.04 for a small, open skiff in estimated 48 mph. winds (41.73 knots), he calculated that during the height of the storm that the skiffs could have drifted away from shore at the surprising rate of 2.96 mph. Helmer's estimate that he drifted 40 to 50 miles from shore "into the shipping lanes" is correct.

* * *

It was at an annual *Gales of November* conference in Duluth that I talked with Thunder Bay fireman Dave Grant and wondered aloud how a fisherman could stay warm during those remarkable hours in his skiff when ice formed on him and his boat. I had first met Dave on Thompson Island, at the mouth of Thunder Bay, Canada, after I arrived after my own adventures during the notorious Green Storm. Dave, who was attending the conference with his boating friend, Clive Dudley, told me that in the winter, Thunder Bay firemen routinely are coated with spray atop their ladders when fighting fires and their garments become sheeted with ice.

But this was beneficial, Dave said, since "the ice keeps you warm." However, Dave explained, another fireman sometimes has to climb the ladder to chop you free.

The insulating properties of several inches of ice covering him might have been one of the reasons the Old Man's said he was relatively warm during his long ordeal on the lake .

*   *   *

I want to thank the North Shore Commercial Fishing Museum, Tofte, MN, and its devoted secretary, Mary Alice Hansen. The Fishing Museum is a modern replica of fishing houses that once stood high atop the bluffs overlooking Superior from which North Shore fishermen went out on their sometimes incredible voyages. The Museum has collected and preserved boats, engines, nets and other memorabilia of a bygone age on Superior, well worth noting and remembering. Of particular interest is the Museum's recording of Helmer Aakvik, his voice low and undramatic, as he recounts his hours on the lake when he tried to rescue his partner, Carl Hammer. The Fishing Museum's video includes some old photographs of Aakvik and other fishermen.

I recommend a visit. Look over the boat slide and down the rocks to an awaiting Lake Superior and doff your hat in respect.

*   *   *

Not long before his death, Aakvik was photographed standing beside his wooden coffin along the cliffs overlooking Lake Superior. He had returned to die beside the lake he had known for 66 years.

He almost didn't make it back. Several years earlier, when he was ill with cancer, Aakvik and his wife had moved from their rustic cabin to his wife's brother's home near Clarksfield, MN.

As the Old Man became aware his end was near, he returned to his beloved North Shore and what he considered "his home," Lake Superior. Calmly preparing for his end, he kept his specially built coffin in his home, he said, so it would be ready when his time came.

He told people that he had nothing to worry about. "I got my boat ready for the trip," he said. He had tried his coffin on for size and declared that "everything was just right."

"I've seen quite a bit in my lifetime," he said, adding, "It's about time to go aloft, like the old sailors say." He looked forward to calm seas ahead.

Three weeks after he returned to Superior, he died. He was buried at Trinity Lutheran Church Cemetery, located in the heavily wooded hills overlooking Superior. He was 90.

3: The Lost Schooner

MY DISCOVERY of the *Clark* came about by accident. I had been traveling through Wisconsin when I began reading *WoodenBoat* magazine. Fascinated, I drove my car into Menominee, MI, to see the old schooner for myself.

"Down by the waterfront," one woman told me. I found the boat at sunset, her masts illuminated eerily in the blood-red dying rays of the sun. The waterfront location was within an improvised fortress of plywood and scraps of lumber. The museum's doors were locked.

The next morning, I was the first one there, with my wife, Loris, and son, Will. Propped up not very successfully in a dirt berth lay the old schooner. She was weathered gray, her wooden hull strakes cracking and her hull hogged. A sag in the middle, with the ends uplifted, was evident.

Even so, the *Clark* was a real treasure – not a replica, not a working imitation of anything, but a real boat snatched from her watery grave and more than 150 years old. I put out my hand to her old hull. In the morning sun, it felt warm and inviting.

As I walked on board, the deck seemed more than a little springy underfoot, but I figured that if they let people onboard, the boat wouldn't be unsafe. But in the aft cabin, the floor was not just springy, it was mushy – sure signs of rot. I backed out, warily. I had nearly put my foot through.

She seemed to have been built with the best of everything from her era and that was the secret of her long underwater life. From the northern Great Lakes forests had come fine old-growth oak and I could only marvel at the white oak (not red oak) planks that sometimes ran as long as 70 feet, virtually unobtainable for boat building today.

She was intended as a fast schooner and built to keep working for a long life, even though just a few voyages in those days would make back her cost.

Frank Hoffmann remained madly enthralled with his dream. "She'll sail again," he told me. She never did. After 25 years on land, she ended ground up by a bulldozer blade.

* * *

I am deeply indebted to Bernie Bloom and Dick Boyd (now Dr. R. J. Boyd, PhD., with Inland Sea Consulting), who provided many insights into their dives on the *Clark* and the *Jennibel* as well as their work with Frank Huffmann.

I knew a little about that unfettered age of sport diving – I had been a SCUBA diver on Lake Superior in the late 1950s and early 60's, when many shipwrecks were discovered. In those days, a diver bold enough to get down to a wreck could remove any "souvenir." Underwater archeology was an infant discipline.

Dr. Boyd had approached the states of Wisconsin and Michigan for advice, aid or scientific expertise as the divers' salvage plans were formulated. "Although officials were very interested in the project," Dr. Boyd said, "they had no money or personnel to assist us. In fact there was no one on either state's staff who had any experience in underwater archeology." He added, "Fortunately, Jim Quinn, a diver and director of Green Bay's Neville Public Museum, freely gave us what archeological help and advice he could muster."

Dr. Boyd was with Hoffmann from the early days and dove with him on the *Jennybel* within 48 hours after the "pirate divers" had attempted to raise her. She had broken in half after their unfortunate salvage failure. "The broken hull was still settling in many places and made strange creaking and groaning noises through the black water," he said. "It truly sounded as though the vessel was emitting its final death rattle...making for a very spooky dive, to say the least."

* * *

The final identification of the *Clark* took considerable research. "Proof of identity was pretty much indirect and circumstantial," Dr. Boyd said, and came in three parts, largely through the work of Bob Olmstead, who was the group's principal researcher: 1/ Newspaper reports on the sinking of the *Clark* gave considerable detail and a precise location of the event. "Thorough research revealed that NO other vessel matching that description had been lost in that vicinity and time period," Dr. Boyd said. The *Oconto Pioneer, Milwaukee Daily News, Racine Advocate, Milwaukee Sentinel,* and *Green Bay Advocate* all had coverage of the sinking. 2/ A small copper plate was found in the forward crew's quarters, which was identified as a personal stencil which read: Mich. Cray, Toronto, C.W. Dr. Boyd said, "Research showed that Michael J. Cray was a survivor of the *Alvin Clark.* He was born in Toronto in 1843 and found his way to the United States, where he served one year in the Union Army during 1862-63. U.S. Army buttons were also found aboard the sunken vessel." 3/ A personal locket found in a ditty bag on the *Clark,* which was traced to a sailor in Racine who had spent most of that decade sailing aboard the *Clark* and no other vessel.

Dr. Boyd told me that a name board was never found on the vessel nor any identification number "since that system did not begin until about 1855, long after the *Clark* was built." Many vessels, he said, had their names painted on and the earliest ones had their names inside the bow rails. "If the *Clark* had a painted -on identification, it did not survive a century of submersion." He added, "Since the schooner was often used to run contraband lumber cargos, it well may be that the ship displayed no obvious identification or that it was entirely removable."

"This lack of identification is not a rare event with shipwrecks," Dr. Boyd explained. "In my 50 years of diving, I have been on numerous wrecks that held no identification of any kind, and this was especially true for schooners and other small sailing vessels. I suspect this was because that data was painted on or was put on boards, which were lost during the sinking. For whatever reason, 'nameless shipwrecks' are pretty common."

*   *   *

To keep trespassing divers and souvenir hunters away, volunteers were on guard almost daily from morning to sunset and the Menominee County Sheriff's Marine Patrol frequently patrolled the dive site. It came as a surprise that after the *Clark* was raised, a number of sport divers came to the museum, with their hats in their hands, so to speak, and a parcel or two under their arms or in the backs of their pickup trucks.

It turned out, Dr. Boyd said, that "even with our heightened security, some divers had risked night descents and also dives during stormy weather to see the wreck and to snatch a souvenir."

Their visits to the museum were their way of paying homage to the *Clark* and bringing part of the lost schooner back "home."

*　　*　　*

For a look at the *Clark* during her final days, go to the web site *www.dlumberyard.com* and click on the *Alvin Clark.* Here are photographs of the crumbling old schooner during her last years. Model boatbuilders made scale measurements and in their step-by-step building of a miniature vessel, you can feast your eyes on the *Clark's* remarkably robust construction and beauty of lines. Your sense of loss will grow and deepen.

4: The Last Race of the *Edmund Fitzgerald*

 I WAS REMINDED of just how overwhelming the forces must have been to sink a ship of the *Edmund Fitzgerald's* size and construction when I examined the *William A. Irvin*, docked on the harbor side of the Duluth, MN, Arena Auditorium. An outstanding floating museumship, the 610-foot *Irwin* was an ore carrier and the flagship of the United State Steel's Pittsburgh Steamship Company, and sailed on the Great Lakes from 1938 until she was retired and moved to Duluth in 1986. With her screen bulkheads removed, I walked through the big ore-carrier's cargo holds, which lay beneath the waterline. Later, I clambered up the steps into the aft spar deck and entered the crew dining room and galley. From there, I made my way into the gleaming engine room, about five stories high, and leaned over the polished brass rails. Below, I saw the main turbines and the huge propeller shaft.

This is a huge, massively built ship whose size emphasized to me how different the world of the aft section crew was than that of wheelhouse. Here the boat's operation was up close and personal: in a hard turn, the crew could hear the groan of the rudder in the water and actually feel the slight flexing and movement of the hull. Here the crew could feel the bite of the 16-foot wheel as it thrashed through the seas at about 60 revolutions per minute that even in relatively calm seas made the aft section vibrate and fill with a heavy rumble, like a waterfall. No doubt about it: The aft section men quickly knew of anything wrong with their boat.

My visit aboard the *Irwin* brought back memories of a voyage on the North Atlantic Ocean. In a late May crossing, we were bound out of New York Harbor for Germany when a storm arose. The steel troopship was battered on its port side with heavy waves, some perhaps 20 feet in height. Belowdecks, where I was berthed with my Armored Infantry battalion, the steel hull clicked, groaned, roared, boomed and howled. I had been amazed at the sounds of the hull working in the storm's waves. Belowdecks, the metal hull had been alive with noises.

I wondered what it had been like in the *Fitz,* a tired older boat with a loose keel that complained to her crew even in quiet weather? As I stood in the *Irwin's* engine room, my mind drifted uneasily to that storm when even the *Fitz's* huge propeller bounced in and out of the water. I thought of the thunder-like noise; I thought of the groaning sounds of the hull flexing like a springboard. Looking upward, I thought of water cascading in as waves overran the sinking hull.

There are some questions that still haunt me. What happened in those fateful moments after the aft section went under? Images came uneasily to mind of the engine room moving sharply downward and twisting upside down, in a huge fall. Then came the darkness, the cold and the terrible waiting.

5: The Passion of Mike Plant

A T A TIME when no other American sailor had made inroads into solo around-the-world racing, a field that was dominated by European sailing professionals, Mike Plant had brilliantly emerged as a champion. The fact that he built his own boat in his first races only emphasized his status as a sailor who could do almost anything and beat the odds through sheer determination and resourcefulness. Mike was a hero and an inspiration to other sailors.

His friends who openly shared their

feelings and memories with me brought home what a loss Mike's untimely death was. A remarkable mariner whose future lay brightly ahead, he eagerly and boldly embraced the newest boat technology that was creating lighter and faster boats. *Coyote* was created out of the wave of the future and she was a remarkable and innovative new boat. Though *Coyote* was launched only weeks before she had to take her maiden run across the North Atlantic, the call of the sea and the lure of the race inexorably drew him and he took a chance on a newly built boat with some untried structural elements. A friend gave me this advice: Never go to sea in a new boat. Only go in an old boat.

*   *   *

The Coast Guard investigation turned up the problem of vibrations emanating from the keel's foil and bulb. After *Coyote* reached a speed of about 9 knots, the report said, vibrations created a humming sound "that could be heard throughout the vessel, and, the vibrations were strong enough to be felt by those aboard. As the vessel increased its speed the sound made by the vibrations would change."

The Coast Guard report explained that this is a common problem on racing yachts like the *Coyote,* but that the vibrations do not occur on all vessels nor can they be predicted during the vessel's design phase. The vibrations are not normally detected until the vessel is put through sea trials.

The report said that the vibrations were caused by the keel's foil as it cut through the water as "the leading edge of the foil splits the water so that it flows down both the port and starboard sides of the foil. At the trailing edge of the foil the two streams of water merge together again. It is the two streams of water meeting at the trailing edge of the foil that causes the foil to vibrate slightly." The problem could have been solved, the report stated, "by beveling one side of the foil's trailing edge at a 45 degree angle while leaving the other side of the foil's trailing edge untouched. This alters the flow of water around the trailing edge of the foil enough to eliminate the vibrations." The report concluded that the boat builder offered to bevel the trailing edge of *Coyote's* foil, "but Plant declined to have it done."

Probably, Mike figured it was a small problem and he just didn't have the time. But it's possible that the vibration in the keel, as outlined by the Coast Guard report, became a mask for a fatal flaw in *Coyote*. Had the chemical bonding for the plate that held the 8,400-pound ballast bulb been even microscopically broken earlier by efforts to twist the big racer free during her groundings, the keel's inherent vibrations and humming noises would have covered up any warning noises down below.

As the Coast Guard report stated, it was possible that the plate's epoxy bonding was fractured after the grounding in Chesapeake Bay, though the plate continued to be held in place by the encapsulating carbon fiber wraps. These are strong materials, used widely in military and aircraft construction. But if the plate were no longer bonded, it would have been free to vibrate as the sailboat slammed into the Gulf Stream's storm waves. Over a period of time, the vibration could have increased with the friction between the graphite and the steel, enlarging the gap. Probably, Mike did not notice anything amiss above the normal vibrations emitted by the keel and the noises within the hull, at least not at first when he began his voyage.

After he got further into the North Atlantic, he probably had some indication something was wrong down below, but by that time it would have been too late to turn back. He probably did what most sailors would have done: hope everything would hold together and kept on sailing.

*   *   *

My special thanks to Mary and Frank Plant, of Plymouth, MN, for their help and assistance in the development of this chapter. Mary graciously took me into their home and showed me the charts she and friends of Mike's had developed as an aid to locating her missing son, and she shared considerable information with me. Remarkably, those charts had come astoundingly close to identifying the area where the overturned *Coyote* was ultimately found much later.

In their efforts to get help for their missing son, they came to realize that the EPIRB he was carrying had not been duly registered and for a number of reasons, prompt rescue action was not taken. Recognizing the need for proper registration of EPIRB's, the Plants and others began a campaign for mandatory registration of the units at the time they are sold. There was a lot of initial support for this effort, but ultimately, registration at point of sale was never legislated into law. However, as the result of the tragedy of Mike Plant, the necessity of quick registration has become a high priority for boaters. Boater's organizations, such as BoatUS, now rents high-quality EPIRB's for short-term use and pays particular attention to get them properly registered.

My thanks to sailmaker Dan Neri, who spent time aboard *Coyote* with Mike, and who was most helpful in explaining *Coyote's* remarkable sailing abilities and performance. Thanks also to marine photographer Billy Black, another friend of Mike's, for his memorable photo of Mike smiling as he looked back over the stern of *Coyote*.

Special thanks to *Cruising World* Editor Herb McCormick, who was kind enough to share information including the February 1993 *Cruising World* special report he wrote, *Gone to Sea*, which was one of the best and most complete magazine articles ever written on the loss of Mike Plant. Herb had the privilege of spending some time with Mike onboard *Coyote*.

Thanks also to Capt. Thom Burns, of *Northern Breezes* sailing magazine and a fellow member of the Mike Plant committee, who provided many valuable insights for this chapter.

6: The Day All Hell Broke Loose

BOATERS HAVE ASKED why my boat capsized only so far on its side but didn't roll over all the way. In the storm, *Persistence* had tipped over so far she seemed beyond the point of recovery, teetering with her mast tip actually in the water, with water sloshing up the centerboard case.

In the incredible winds, the boat had accelerated wildly and had her bow forced downward into the water, causing a semi-pitchpole. *Persistence* had stopped abruptly and I had been pitched headfirst and forward down into the cabin. As I lay partly dazed, I was aware of my boat gathering force and whipping down on her starboard side, as if she were rolling over all the way. I had a flash vision of being trapped upside down, in a dark hull, and swept out further onto stormy Superior. But then a little miracle had happened. The hull seemed to bounce – I could feel it – and then it partly righted itself.

My boat was taking care of both of us, just as I hoped she would, when I built her. I had been concerned about capsizing in a centerboard boat without a ballast keel and my solution was several small innovations. In extreme conditions, I couldn't prevent her from going partly over to one side, but I could help her not go bottom up. I thought I knew a way.

My revelation had come during an adventure when I had been out in a daysailor with friends on a small lake and we capsized under wind pressure that we had not able to release. Slowly, the boat partly immersed on her starboard side and lay with her mast flat on the water. For several moments, her mast gurgled and spit out air, taking on water. Then the boat turned turtle and we were hanging onto a capsized boat, whose mast pointing downward, sails attached. We righted her without problems using the centerboard for leverage, but there were three of us (as well as a dog), and actually, it had been fun.

But on *Persistence's* Superior voyages, I figured it'd be best not to go over all the way in these chill waters. To prevent a total capsize, I had squirted expanding foam sealant into the top of the mast. figuring that the hardened foam would give *Persistence* some buoyancy. At least if her mast tip dunked into the water, it would not fill up with water and make her turn turtle the way the little daysailor did.

During my capsize, *Persistence* had performed just as I had anticipated. Her foamed mast tip dipped into the water and started on its way down, when the buoyancy in the mast forced the boat back up to an angle where the boat's righting motion could take over. The mast's buoyancy had given my little boat her "bounce back."

Another help to recovery were the large rubrails I had constructed. Many sailboats have rubrails of plastic or rubber on the hull's sides to ward off contact with docks or other boats, but I built *Persistence's* rubrails out of buoyant Sitka Spruce. These were like little wooden "life rafts" around the hull and helped *Persistence* right herself, without going over.

Also, I had built *Persistence's* cabin sides nearly out to the edge of the deck. Unlike those boats with cabins set back from their sides, my little boat did not go up on edge, and, finally flop over on her cabin top, in an upside-down capsize. When the starboard side of *Persistence's* cabin went under water, it helped give the boat additional buoyancy and balance. I also had built the cabin walls as strong as my hull, so that if the cabin ever did go underwater, nothing would break. Nothing did.

*   *   *

It was only after I returned to my home in Shoreview, MN, and began reading newspapers that had been saved for me that I came to realize the full infamy of the storm. The July 4, 1999, Independence Day Storm had been severe. News articles told how the storm had devastated about a half a million acres damaging 25 million trees in the Boundary Waters Canoe Area Wilderness (BWCAW). Trees had been broken like so many matchsticks and were stacked 10-feet high in places. It was one of the "largest North American forest disturbances in recorded history." Newspapers called it "the storm of the century."

Initially, I assumed that the winds were powerful straight line blasts, but I could not figure out how straight line winds would pin my boat on its side and keep it there. Something was not quite right.

To get a first-hand look, I drove my 4 x 4 through some of the devastated areas and saw not only tops of hills scraped bare of trees but even an entire valley that had been scooped out. Straight-line winds would no do that. To be certain, there was a lot of wind up here. One newspaper said that gusts reached 110 mph. Another reported 115 mph. I remained puzzled.

*   *   *

One day, I received an e-mail from Bob John, a former lead forecaster from the Storm Prediction Center in Norman, OK, who was developing a web site, *About Derechos*, (www.spc.noaa. gov/misc/AbtDerechos) and with his help, I learned more about the July 4, 1999 "green storm" I had survived.

Derechos (pronounced "day-ray-cho) are violent, big superstorms produced by long-lived thunderstorm complexes that barnstorm across regions with straight line winds of 60 to 100 mph.. To be a derecho, a storm must both have severe winds of more than 58 mph. over a path of at least 280 miles (about the distance from New York City to Boston).

Now came the information that made my skin crawl: Out of these high-speed superstorms comes not only straight line winds but even faster downbursts and microbursts of heavy, chill air. These downburst clusters slam downward from the squall line and hug the ground below, blasting anything in their path. As a general rule, says NOAA, these surface winds are likely to be "well in excess perhaps as much as double the gust front speed."

Downbursts were probably what did much of the heavy damage in the BWCAW area and were what had hit me on Superior. I learned that downbursts speed up on water, since there is nothing to obstruct them, such as hills and forests.

In addition to a straight-line winds and dangerous downburst clusters, the derecho poses yet another danger: it is a long-lived storm and may continue on for some distance with its long troughs of intense damage.

On the *About Derechos* web site, I was able to bring up radar imagery which showed the "Green Storm" accelerating and changing into "an extremely dangerous" Type 2 bow-echo to the west of my location. Originally, I thought the derecho had begun on somewhere to the northwest of my location and had ended somewhere east of Thunder Bay. But imagery showed the derecho actually continued to roar eastward to Maine and end near the Atlantic coast, a path of destruction nearly 1,500 miles long, with a lifespan of almost 24 hours.

The BWCAW took the worst brunt of the just-formed derecho, with old-growth pines and ancient spruce trees broken like so many matchsticks. Impressive as it was, the July 4, 1999 "Green Storm" derecho was not the strongest derecho ever recorded in recent history. On July 4, 1977, a derecho swept across northern Wisconsin with winds measured at 115 mph. On May 31, 1998, a measured wind gust was recorded at 128 mph. in eastern Wisconsin and gusts were estimated at 130 mph. in Lower Michigan.

The implication is clear: The deadly storms can come out of the sky anywhere over water or land and with very little warning and typically can't be predicted. They are "first worst" storms, with the most severe and usually most dangerous damage occurring during the first minutes.

About a dozen derechos are identified across the U.S. each

year and they also occur in other parts of the world, including the killer storms known as "Nor'westers" in Bangladesh and adjacent portions of India, which may also be progressive derechos.

During the July 4, 1999 derecho,forecasters had been monitoring a large, severe storm from the eastern edges of Minnesota, but as the storm passed to their north, "barreling toward the Boundary Waters, the wind signature diminished on the screen," said the *Earth Bulletin* of the American Museum of Natural History (http://earthbulletin.amnh.org/ D/2/2/) on its *Derecho!* page. Meteorologists could still make out the bow-echo reflection of raindrops on the ground, so they had a good idea of where the gust front was located, though they could no longer determine actual speeds at ground level. As it turned out, the *Bulletin* reported, that was precisely the moment when the storm evolved into "a full-blown derecho." The weather station was the last radar station along the path to northern Minnesota and the last to see the storm before it turned into a derecho."

The specific warning of a derecho never came. Minutes later, it hit me.

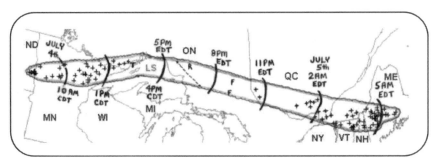

Path of the July 4, 1999 Derecho that engulfed the author on Superior (NOAA illustration). The derecho extended into Lake Superior and swept eastward across the U.S. until it ended in Maine. The crosses mark the areas of the most intense damage, where downbursts could have hit as high as 115 - 130 mph.

INDEX

MORE ADVENTURE DEAD

WAKE OF THE GREEN STORM: A SURVIVOR'S TALE

"Recommended" – *The Library Journal*

"Equals any oceanic adventure" – *The San Diego Log*

"Unusually fine craftsmanship." – *Stillwater Gazette*

"Here's some reading for a dark and stormy night, but only if you are safely tied to the dock. "

On July 4, 1999, Marlin Bree was caught in "the storm of the century," a rare progressive derecho with downbursts clocked at 115 mph. Without warning, the lone sailor and his 20-foot wooden boat were caught in a wall of wind. *Wake of the Green Storm* tells of the author's fight to survive on the stormy open waters of Lake Superior. Interspersed with Bree's own adventures are tales of other boater's storm experiences, including the destruction of the *Grampa Woo,* and the survival of a lone man drifting on an ice-covered life raft. Here are remarkable stories of dangerous storms, shipwrecks as well as a voyage through the rugged and picturesque northern archipelago of the world's largest freshwater lake. "Incredible."– *Great Lakes Cruiser.* ISBN1-892147-04-1 / trade paperback, 6 x 9 inches, 48 charts, illustrations and drawings. 224 pages. **$13.95US / $18.95 Canada**

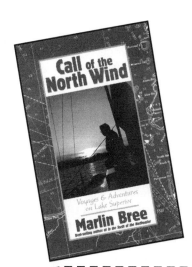

Photo / Will Bree

ABOUT THE AUTHOR

Aboard his home-built epoxy/wood sloop, Marlin Bree feels that wooden boats are like family and friends: "They don't get older, they only get better." He is the author of four nonfiction boating books: *In the Teeth of the Northeaster, Call of the North Wind, Wake of the Green Storm,* and *The Boat Log & Record.* With sailor Gerry Spiess, he co-authored the national best-seller, *Alone Against the Atlantic.* Bree's writings have appeared in numerous boating publications, including *Cruising World, Soundings, The Ensign, Northern Breezes* and *Small Craft Advisor.* A former newsman with the *Minneapolis Star Tribune,* Bree is a past president of the Minnesota Press Club and is a member of Boating Writers International and the Author's Guild.He is the recipient of numerous writing awards, including the 2004 West Marine Writer's Award, the top honor Boating Writer's International bestows upon a boating writer. He is profiled in *Who's Who in America.* He lives with his wife, Loris, son, Will, and ocicat, Tico, in their home in Shoreview, Minnesota.

Visit Marlin's web site at *www.marlinbree.com*
for more information and color photographs of his boat.
His site contains a hot link to his e-mail address.
He is always happy to hear from fellow sailors and boat builders.